JOHN B. KEANE is one of Ireland's most popul[...] [...] recognised as a major Irish playwright. He has written many bestsellers including *Letters of a Successful T.D.*, *Letters of an Irish Parish Priest*, *Letters of an Irish Publican*, *Letters of a Matchmaker*, *Letters of a Love Hungry Farmer*, *The Gentle Art of Matchmaking*, *Irish Short Stories*, *More Irish Short Stories*, *The Bodhrán Maker* and *Man of the Triple Name*. His plays include *Sharon's Grave*, *Many Young Men of Twenty*, *The Man from Clare*, *The Year of the Hiker*, *Moll*, *The Change in Mame Fadden*, *Values*, *The Crazy Wall* and *The Buds of Ballybunion*.

The Field

AND OTHER IRISH PLAYS

John B. Keane

ROBERTS RINEHART PUBLISHERS

ISBN 1-879373-98-x
Library of Congress Catalog Card Number 94-66095

Published in the U.S. and Canada by
Roberts Rinehart Publishers
Post Office Box 666, Niwot, Colorado 80544

First published in Ireland in 1990 by Mercier Press

Printed in the United States of America
Distributed by Publishers Group West

Front cover illustration from a photograph by Tom Kelly

Contents

Introduction

At the beginning and at the end, things often look the same. Things begin in confusion and end in confusion. And so it is appropriate that the plays of John B. Keane which dramatised so many of the tensions of the new era inaugurated in the 1960s in Ireland should be enjoying new life at the end of that era. When Keane started to write *Sive* in the late 1950s emigration had reached 50,000 a year and rural Ireland was facing momentous changes: industrialisation, the end of the extended family, new attitudes to sexuality. Now, thirty years later, emigration is back to nearly 50,000 a year and many of the changes which Keane's best plays explored have proved not to be the solutions we thought they might be. The times and the questions may be different, but just as Keane needed to explore those changes from one end, so we need to explore them from the other.

It is in this context that Ben Barnes has been re-exploring and re-defining Keane's major plays — *Sive, The Field* and *Big Maggie*. Given that his productions of these plays represent such a belated recognition on the part of the Abbey to Keane's importance, Ben Barnes might have been content with an act of homage, a respectful welcoming of these plays into the national canon, long after they had been accepted by theatre audiences around the country as plays which spoke to them and about them. But theatre doesn't work like that — mere respect is the cold hand of death on a play. Barnes has treated the plays like new works, approaching them with a clarity and vigour that has sought to root them in the world in which they make sense. And John B. Keane has responded with new writing, including, for the production of *Big Maggie*, a new ending.

Because the form of his plays tends to be quite simple, because he deals with the rough passions of sex and violence and greed, because he has continued to work at his trade of bar-keeping in Listowel, there has been a tendency to see John B. Keane's plays as in some way primitive or naive. And indeed in the way they draw on folk tradition and religious conflicts of good and evil, they do evoke a primitive power that is readily understandable to anyone in rural Ireland. But while staying in touch with this power, Ben Barnes' productions have also exposed the sharpness and subtlety of *Sive, The Field* and *Big Maggie*. He has shown them to be plays that are less about a mythic clash of good and evil and more about the human dilemmas that confront ordinary people in times of change.

Sive, *The Field* and *Big Maggie* all have a fearful visceral force about them, but they are also thoughtful and keenly-observed dramatisations of social change and it has been Ben Barnes' achievement to restore that dimension. Mena in *Sive* may be a bad and greedy woman prepared to sell-off her foster-child for financial gain, but in Catherine Byrne's performance she was also, as we could begin to see, a woman desperately trying to come to terms with the coming change, to get her family in shape for the fast-approaching future, to do the best for her husband and herself.

Even more startlingly, the Barnes' production of *The Field* managed to turn that most demonic of modern Irish theatrical characters, the Bull McCabe, into a comprehensible individual rather than an ogre from the depths. For some, Niall Tóibín's performance was a reduction of 'The Bull', for me, it was a deepening. And it worked because the production was so firmly rooted in a sense of social change, of the change from a rustic world to an industrialised country. Instead of being the theatrical equivalent of the Evil Baron tying the helpless maiden to the train tracks, The Bull became a man defending what he had reason to think of as his by the lights of the old order, not understanding that the old order had changed. Instead of being a melodrama, the play became something very like a tragedy.

Big Maggie was the logical play with which to follow these two successes, because Maggie is a kind of cross between Mena and The Bull with much of The Bull's brutal scheming energy allied to Mena's belief that she is acting for the best. Like both of them, she, too, is caught between an old world and a new one, and her plight is tragic. Unlike either of them her battle-ground is sexual rather than economic. Born and raised with one set of social values, she now has to cope with another. Brenda Fricker's superb performance as Maggie in Ben Barnes' production showed just how close to the nerve-ends of the nation her struggle remains. As in all tragedies, the most she can hope to win is self-awareness, and this, in the new ending to the play, she gains. That gift of self-awareness is one that these plays now bring to Irish society, going into the uncertainties of the 1990s, with renewed and clarified power.

FINTAN O' TOOLE

Sive

This edited two-act version of *Sive* was first presented in the Abbey Theatre, Dublin on Thursday 13 June 1985.

NANNA GLAVIN	Marie Kean
MENA GLAVIN	Catherine Byrne
SIVE	Maeve Germaine
THOMASHEEN SEÁN RUA	Dónall Farmer
MIKE GLAVIN	John Olohan
LIAM SCUAB	Sean Campion
SEÁN DÓTA	Micheál Ó Briain
PATS BOCOCK	Eamon Kelly
CARTHALAWN	Macdara Ó Fátharta

DIRECTOR   Ben Barnes
DESIGNER   Monica Frawley
LIGHTING DESIGN   Tony Wakefield
MUSIC   Roger Doyle

Sive was first produced by the Listowel Amateur Drama Group at Walsh's Ballroom, Listowel on 2 February 1959.

ACT ONE

Scene 1

[The kitchen is poorly furnished, with an open hearth on its left wall. A door leads to a bedroom at the left side of the hearth. On the wall facing the audience there is a small window, and a door leads to the yard at the front of the house.

A large dresser, filled with ware in its upper half, stands between the door and the window. A third door is in the right wall of the kitchen with a small working-table at one side. Overhead a mirror hangs. Under the table are two buckets and a basin. A 20-gallon creamery tank stands between the door and the table with a half-filled sack of meal and a half-sack of flour.

A larger table stands in the middle of the floor. There are six súgán chairs; two beside the table; two by the fire; the others on either side of the dresser.

In the hearth a black skillet hangs from a crane and a large black kettle rests in a corner. An enamel bucket of drinking water is on the table.

The time is late evening of a bitter March day, in the late 1950s.

An old woman bent forward with age, dressed in black, sits near the fire surreptitiously smoking a clay pipe. She is NANNA GLAVIN, *mother of the man of the house. She holds the tongs, idly gathering the fire; with the other hand she conveys the pipe continuously between lap and mouth.*

When she hears the door latch lifting the tongs falls in her haste to conceal the pipe. A great quantity of red petticoat, and long boots tied up to her shins, are revealed when she lifts her skirt to hide the pipe.

Her skirts are hardly in place again, when another woman enters. The newcomer is strong, well-proportioned, hard-featured, in her early forties: her hair raven-black tied sharply in a bun gives the front of her head the appearance of being in want of hair, or being in a coif. She is MENA, *wife of the man of the house]*

Mena:	There's a smell of smoke!
Nanna:	*[Crossly]* 'Tis the way you left the fire when you went out.
Mena:	Not turf smoke, oul' woman, tobacco smoke!
Nanna:	Tobacco smoke how are you? *[NANNA seizes the tongs and belabours the fire]*

Mena: In the name of all that's dead and gone, wouldn't you take out your pipe and smoke it not be humpin' yourself there like a cat stealin' milk?

[MENA bends to take one of the buckets from under the working table. She puts it between her boots and pours water from the full enamel drinking bucket into it. She replaces the enamel drinking bucket]

Nanna: *[Irritably]* Such clatter!

[MENA scoops several fistfuls of meal from the bag into the bucket]

Mena: No clatter unless 'tis your own. Wouldn't you give over talkin' and take out your pipe *[wearily]* and not be hiding it when we walk in and out of the kitchen?

Nanna: Am I to be scolded, night and day, in my own house? Ah! 'twas a sore day to me my son took you for a wife. What a happy home we had before you came into it! Fitter for you be having three or four children put from you at this day of your life.

Mena: I had my fortune; 'twasn't for the want of a roof over my head that I came here. I could have done better if I bided by time. *[Lifts bucket and turns to door]*

Nanna: We all know what you could do, girl, and the stock you came from . . . and the cabin you came out of! *[Laughs a little forcefully]* Where ye used to drink yeer tay out of jampots for the want of cups. Oh, indeed, you needn't tell me about yourself. A nice bargain you were!

Mena: You have nothing else to do but talk. Saying your prayers you should be, at this hour of your days, instead of cackling with your bad tongue . . . Where was your poor amadán of a son before I came here? Pulling bogdeal out of the ground with a jinnet, going around like a half-fool with his head hanging by him . . . you give me the puke with your grandeur. Take out your dirty dúidín of a pipe and close your gob on it, woman. I have something else to do beside arguing with you.

[MENA lifts the latch to go out. As she does so, the door opens and a pretty young girl enters. She is aged about 18 and wears a grey tweed coat, a little too small for her. A flimsy scarf covers her head. She carries a satchel, filled with books, in her hand. Her name is SIVE. When she enters, MENA closes the door and looks at SIVE piercingly. SIVE puts her satchel on the large table, aware of MENA'S eyes upon her back]

Sive: I was held up after leaving the village. The front wheel of the bicycle went flat on me, and to crown my misfortune didn't I get a slow puncture in the other wheel. 'Tis the tyres that are worn. I was lucky to meet the master on the road. He gave me a lift as far as the end of the bóithrín. *[She unties her scarf]*

Mena: Schoolmasters and motor-cars, and I suppose you expect me to have a hot dinner ready for you any minute of the day you decide to come home.

Sive: Oh, no! . . . we had a cookery class at the convent today, all the girls got dinner there. We had fricassee with dartois for dessert. It was lovely!

Mena: Saints preserve us! Out working with a farmer you should be my girl, instead of getting your head filled with high notions. You'll come to no good either, like the one that went before you!

[MENA lifts the bucket and goes out. SIVE takes off her coat and holds it over her arm. Underneath she wears a brown schoolgirl uniform with white collar attached]

Sive: What does she mean, Gran. The one that went before. Who was she referring to?

Nanna: There's no meaning to that woman's blather! *[Lifts her skirt and puts her pipe into her mouth]* Quenched! . . . bad skewer to her gone out!

Sive: She meant my mother, didn't she, Gran?

Nanna: *[Takes box of matches from her pocket and lights her pipe]* 'Sha your mother.

Sive: Well, Gran, it was my mother, wasn't it? What did she mean?

Nanna: Your mother, the Lord have mercy on her, was my daughter. She wouldn't dare to draw down her name . . . it was only poison prattle, child; wind and steam. Isn't she always at it. 'Tis the disease in her system. If she didn't let it out of her mouth, 'twould break out in boils and sores all over her. You're worse, to take notice of her!

Sive: *[Lays her coat over books on table and sits on its edge facing grandmother]* Gran all I know about my mother is that she died when I was a baby. Any time I've asked questions about her you've all put me off and told me you didn't know or that you had forgotten . . . and my father . . . you say he was drowned, no more. What I want to know is what sort of man was he. Was he funny; was he handsome? Why wasn't he here by my mother's side when I was born or what kind of a father was he that he left her to suffer alone?

Nanna: He was in England. He couldn't be here, could he, when he was there. He was drowned, the poor boy, a few days after you were born. Coal-mining he was, when the waters rushed in and trapped him. *[Reflective sadness]* Away over in England.

Sive: What was I like when I was born? Am I like my father now or like my mother?

Nanna: Questions! Questions! Nothing but questions! You were a fine common lump of a baby! I remember well the night you were born. The doctor came in his new motor-car from the village. I remember well to see the two roundy balls of fire coming up the bóithrín. The old people swore it was the devil but sure it was only the two headlamps of the car shining in the darkness. *[Draws on her pipe fruitlessly]* Devil take the tobacco they're making these days!

Sive: Tell me more about my mother, Gran! She was pretty, wasn't she?

Nanna: *[With regret]* She was pretty, too pretty. *[Shakes her head]* She was handsome, God rest her.

[The kitchen door opens noiselessly and MENA stands framed in it without speaking. She is unnoticed by SIVE and NANNA. She carries the empty bucket]

Sive: Go on, Gran! Tell me more! You must have so many stories about my mother when she was young.

Nanna: What more is there to tell?

[She lifts her head, looks past SIVE to the door and tries to indicate to SIVE that MENA is at the door. She hides her pipe hurriedly.

Suddenly SIVE understands and looks behind her in bewilderment. She comes to her feet quickly]

Mena: 'Tis a wonder you took your backside from the table where people do be eating. Is that what you're learning at the convent?

[Abashed, SIVE takes her coat and books from the table. MENA puts bucket under the working-table]

Mena: Your uncle and I work ourselves to the marrow of the bones to give you schooling and the minute I turn my back you're cohackling with that oul' boody woman in the corner. *[To NANNA]* Some day that pipe will take fire where you have it hidden and you'll go off in a big black ball of smoke and ashes.

Nanna: *[Slowly]* If I do, 'tis my prayer that the wind will blow me in your direction and I'll have the satisfaction of taking you with me. Aha, you'd burn well, for you're as dry as the hobs of hell inside of you. Every woman of your age in the parish has a child of her own and nothing to show by you.

Mena: Hold your tongue, old woman. How dare you cast your curses inside in my own house. It isn't my fault I have no child. *[Looks meaningly at SIVE]* Enough that had children in their time. I have every right to this house. I paid dear for my share.

Nanna: I was here before you.

Mena: Ah, but you won't be here after me!

Nanna: That is the will of God, woman; not your will.

Mena: *[To SIVE — loudly]* Take your books and get to your room. Is it for ornament you think we are keeping you? I'm sure the nuns would like to hear of your conduct.

[SIVE hurries to the door at right of kitchen. She casts a quick look behind her towards her grandmother as she goes]

Mena: What nonsense have you been filling the girl's head with? She'll be as cracked as the crows if she listens to you; wasting her time when she should be at her studies. When I was her age in my father's house I worked from dawn till dark to put aside my fortune.

Nanna: You should have stayed in your father's house . . . Your father *[derisively]* a half-starved bocock of a beggar with the Spanish blood galloping through his veins like litters of hungry greyhounds.

Mena: *[Threateningly]* Old woman, be careful with your free tongue! 'Twill wither up inside your head. You mind your corner of the house and I'll mind mine. You have great gumption for a woman with nothing.

Nanna: *[Takes the tongs in her hand]* The calves are bawling for their milk.

[NANNA leans on tongs and rises with its support, then lets it fall noisily. She goes after SIVE into room at right of kitchen, ignoring MENA's looks. She walks slightly humped.

When she has left, MENA goes to fire and re-arranges it with the tongs. She goes to the dresser, opens one of the doors and extracts an apron which she ties about her waist. Going to fire she lifts the skillet from the crane and replaces it with the kettle. She uses the hem of her apron to handle both utensils. She goes to the working table and withdraws the second bucket, and listens at door of room where NANNA and SIVE are.

While she is thus occupied there is a faint knock on the kitchen door. She turns instantly, then looks into the mirror and pats her hair hurriedly. She advances a step towards the door]

Mena: Come in, let you!

*[The door opens slowly and a man peers cautiously about
the kitchen. He wears a disfigured felt hat upon unruly
hair and looks as if he had not shaved for a week. He is
shifty-looking, ever on his guard. He is fortyish. He takes
the hat from his head and thrusts it into his coat pocket,
when his eyes rest on MENA. He is THOMASHEEN SEÁN RUA, a
matchmaker]*

Thomasheen: Are you alone, bean a' tí? *[He looks around again]* Or is
there someone with you? *[Very confidential. His voice has
a rasp-like quality with the calculated slow drawl typical
of the south-west]*

Mena: I'm as much alone as ever I'll be. Come in, will you. You
look like a scarecrow there in the doorway.

Thomasheen: Good help us, amn't I like a scarecrow always,
matchmaking and making love between people I spend
my days and no thanks for it.

*[He enters and goes to the fire. He turns his back to it and
lifts the tail of his over-coat to savour the heat. MENA closes
the door and stands at the table]*

Mena: *[Pause]* What is all the secrecy about, Thomasheen. You
look like you have something to tell.

Thomasheen: There's a frightful sting in the air this evening. There is the
sign of rain to the west, God between us and all harm . . .
Is the man of the house within or without?

Mena: He is gone to the village with a rail of banbhs.

Thomasheen: Ah! Great money in banbhs these days. They'll save the
country yet, I may tell you. There's more money in two
banbhs than there is in the making of a match, God help us.

Mena: If you think I can spend the evening listening to buaileam
sciath, you can go the road for yourself. What is it that
brought you? Out with it!

Thomasheen: There is no one with an ear cocked? *[He looks about
suspiciously]*

Mena: The old woman and the girl are below in the room but you can shout to the heavens for all the attention they'll pay to you. If it is after matchmaking you came, boy, you have put pains on your feet for nothing.

Thomasheen: Thomasheen Seán Rua never blisters his feet without cause. There is some one who have a great wish for the young lady, this one they call Sive. 'Tis how he have seen her bicycling to the convent in the village. *[Shakes his head solemnly]* He is greatly taken by her. He have the mouth half-open when he do be talking about her. 'Tis the sign of love, woman!

Mena: Are you by any chance taking leave of your senses, buachall! What is she but a schoolgirl . . . and illegitimate, to crown all! She has no knowledge of her father and the mother is dead with shame out of her the most of 20 years.

Thomasheen: Illegitimate! There is fierce bond to the word and great length to it. Whatever she is, she has the makings of a woman.

Mena: Raiméis! You have great talk.

Thomasheen: Ah! but she have one thing we will never see any more of, God help us . . . she have the youth and the figure and the face to stand over it. 'Tis the youth, blast you, that the old men do be after. 'Tis the heat *[pronounced hait]* before death that plays upon them.

Mena: Old men! What are you saying about old men! *[Her voice rises in volume]*

Thomasheen: Hush, woman! . . . You'll tell the parish! . . . What matter if the girl be what she is, if she had a black face and the hooves of a pony . . . the man I mention is taken with her. He will buy, sell and lose all to have her. He have the wish for the girl.

Mena: *[Suddenly shrewd]* Who has the wish for her?

Thomasheen: No quibble between the pair of us, Mena. Seán Dóta is the man.

Mena: Seán Dóta!

Thomasheen: Hould your hoult, woman! Take heed of what I say. He have the grass of 20 cows. He have fat cattle besides and he have the holding of money.

Mena: He's as old as the hills!

Thomasheen: But he's a hardy thief with the mad mind for women breaking out through him like the tetter with no cure for it. What matter if he is as grey as the goat. There is many a young man after a year of marriage losing his heart for love-making. This man have the temper. He would swim the Shannon for a young wife. He would spoil her, I tell you. There is good reward for all concerned in it. Don't be hasty, to be sorry later.

Mena: You are like all the matchmakers: you will make a rose out of a nettle to make a bargain.

Thomasheen: He have the house to himself — nothing to be done by her only walk in and take charge. There is a servant boy and a servant girl. There is spring water in the back yard, and a pony and trap for going to the village.

Mena: Seán Dóta! *[Reflectively]* The girl hasn't a brown penny to her name.

Thomasheen: No fortune is wanted, I tell you. 'Tis how he will give money to have her.

Mena: He will give money! The devil isn't your master for the red lies. That's the first I ever heard of a farmer giving money instead of looking for it. What will we hear next?

Thomasheen: *[Extends both hands]* 'Tis the ageing blood in the thief . . . Ah! It's an old story, girl. The old man and the young woman. When they get the stroke this way there is no holding them. There is the longing he have been storing away these years past.

Mena: *[Pause]* And you say he would give money for her?

Thomasheen: That my right hand might fall off if he won't! 200 sovereigns for you if the girl will consent.

Mena: *[Suspiciously]* And what is for you? It isn't out of the goodness of yeer heart you are playing your hand.

Thomasheen: There will be a £100 pounds for me.

Mena: £200 . . . she'll scorn him. She has high notions.

Thomasheen: Aye! It won't come aisy. *[He advances a little way towards her and lowers his head to peer at her before going on]* High notions or no high notions, you're the one that can do it. Isn't she a bye-child? . . . Tell her you will bell-rag her through the parish if she goes against you. Tell her you will hunt the oul' woman into the county home. Think of the 200 sovereigns dancing in the heel of your fist. Think of the thick bundle of notes in the shelter of your bussom. It isn't every day of the week £200 will come your way.

Mena: The girl is flighty like a colt. Threats might only make her worse.

Thomasheen: Be silky then, be canny! Take her gentle. Let it out to her by degrees. Draw down the man's name first by way of no harm. You could mention the fine place he have. You could say he would be for the grave within a year or two and that she might pick and choose from the bucks of the parish when he's gone.

Mena: She'll cock her nose at him! . . . 'Tis all love and romancing these days with little thought for comfort or security. *[Pause]* 20 cows and money to burn! *[Reflectively]* She'll do no better for all her airs and graces. Look at the match I made . . . four cows on the side of a mountain and a few acres of bog.

Thomasheen: Remember there's 200 sovereigns staring you in the face if you will be doing your duty by Seán Dóta.

Mena: I will consider *[Pause]* . . . The old woman would be against it. She has the charming of the girl in her hands. They are as thick as thieves, the pair of them.

Thomasheen: Gently will do it, step by step. Show her the chances she will have, the fine clothes and the envy of the neighbours. The house is like a bishop's palace, paper on every wall, and a pot, by all accounts, under every bed. She will have the life of a queen.

Mena: *[Thoughtfully]* And I would be rid of her. And £200 into the bargain. I would!

Thomasheen: And you would be rid of the old woman, too.

Mena: *[Alert]* By what way?

Thomasheen: We will make it a part of the match that she will go with Sive.

Mena: I would be clear and clane of the pair of 'em!

Thomasheen: 'Tis a chance that will not pass the way again.

Mena: Would he take the oul' woman, do you think?

Thomasheen: Do you know the man you have? How many years is Seán Dóta in the world? How many years have he spent searchin' the country for a young woman?

Mena: Will he take the oul' woman or won't he?

Thomasheen: He will have anything, I tell you, if he will get Sive.

Mena: It would be a great day to the house. Years I have suffered with the two of them, always full of hate for me. I would give my right hand to have that oul' hag out of my way.

Thomasheen: Ah, you have no life, God help us, with the worry of them.

Mena: Why should that young rip be sent to a convent every day instead of being out earning with a farmer. Good money going on her because her fool of a mother begged on the deathbed to educate her.

Thomasheen: 'Tis a mortal sin!

Mena: 'Tis worse! 'Tis against nature. She'll have her eyes opened.

Thomasheen: I often wonder how you put up with it at all.

Mena: I won't suffer long more.

Thomasheen: *[Rubs his hands gleefully]* I knew my woman from the start. You must go to the core of the apple to come by the seed.

Mena: Himself? . . . What will he say?

Thomasheen: Aren't ye in the one bed sleeping. Ye will have ye'er own talk. You will come around him aisy. You weren't born a fool, Mena. I know what it is like in the long long hours of the night. I know what it is to be alone in a house when the only word you will hear is a sigh, the sigh of the fire in the hearth dying, with no human words to warm you. I am a single man. *[Deadly serious]* I know what a man have to do who have no woman to lie with him. He have to drink hard, or he have to walk under the black sky when every eye is closed in sleep. Now, with you, there is a difference. You have the man. You have the companion. Sleeping or waking you have your husband in the flesh and bone and there is the one will between ye. You will see that he is of the same word as yourself. Be said by me, leanbh *[ingratiatingly]*, take the rough with the smooth . . . But have your way. Keep the picture of 200 sovereigns in your mind.

Mena: *[Calculatingly]* Aisy said!

Thomasheen: *[Touches her hand]* There is the money to think of. *[He withdraws his hand immediately, and going to window, looks out]* No sign of rail and car. *[He looks at MENA]* Listen, woman, I will call tonight with my man, just as if we were passing the way by chance. Pretend nothing!

[Suddenly the room door at stage right opens noisily and NANNA comes in]

Mena: What is all the fústar for? Is it how the hinges of the door are worn? Or must you make noise wherever you go with the bitterness that's in you?

[NANNA does not answer but goes to the dresser and takes a cup. Slowly, deliberately, she goes to where the milk-tank is. Looking over at THOMASHEEN she lifts its cover and dips cup inside it. She withdraws cup, having filled it, and replaces the cover]

Mena: The top of the tank for her ladyship!

Nanna: Would you see the girl hungry? *[To THOMASHEEN]* I know you, Thomasheen Seán Rua. 'Tis no good that brings you here this day of the week. The mean snap is in you and all that went before you. You'd sell your soul to the devil for a drink of buttermilk.

[THOMASHEEN advances, fists clenched, but holds his tongue. He glares at the old woman, who turns and goes into the room again]

Thomasheen: Ah-ha! Hag! consumptive oul' hag! Seed an' breed of consumptive oul' hags. *[His voice grows high-pitched. To MENA]* Marry the young one and be rid of that oul' devil!

Mena: Huist! . . . I hear the axle of a car on the road . . . 'tis himself coming from the village. *[Becomes flurried]* Clear away with you . . . tonight, mind! I will come around himself in my own time. He has a great love for the few pounds.

Thomasheen: *[Goes to the door and peeps out. Then turns to MENA]* I'll have the old man here by nightfall.

[THOMASHEEN opens the door, looks to left and right and disappears.

   MENA takes three plates and cups from dresser and puts them on table. Goes to the tankard of milk and fills a jug by immersing it. She dries the jug with her apron and fills the three cups with milk. From lower part of dresser she takes three large spoons, and puts them on the table. Between each action she looks out of window. When the door opens, MENA does not turn to look at the new arrival. He is her husband, MIKE GLAVIN. Under his arm he carries a sack partly filled with hay which he puts under the working table. He carries a thonged whip attached to an ash-plant. He is a quiet man, determined of movement. His voice will be studious and calculated]

Mena: You're back!

Mike: Aye!

[He goes immediately to table and sits on the chair nearest to it. The man of the house is home! The woman must become alert in her own way. MIKE searches his right-hand pocket. He withdraws a few currency notes and some silver. He places them on the nearest of the three plates. He smooths the notes awkwardly with his fingers, folds them and begins to count the silver with inexperienced hands. With a single gesture he returns the money to his pocket]

Mena: How much today?

Mike: What have you in the skillet?

Mena: How much money did you make?

Mike: *[He does not move his head]* £16.10s. I gave a crown luck.

Mena: How much for the single banbh?

Mike: 'Twas together I sold them.

Mena: A great day's hire! Will it last?

Mike: 'Twill last! *[Pause]* It makes a great change from beggin' and pinchin' with our craws often only half-filled. Ah! you should see the shopkeepers in the village today. Like singing birds they were, calling out our names when we passed with our loads. *[Noisily]* I mind a day not so long past when they had us by the throats. They wouldn't give the half-sack of flour without money down. The boot is on the other foot now with turf the way it is and pigs and calves fetching the high price. It does the heart good to see the shop-keepers scrapin' and bowin'. Money is the best friend a man ever had. *[He takes off his coat and hangs it from a crook behind kitchen door]*

Mena: We will mind whatever penny we make.

Mike: You may say we'll mind it! *[He puts his hand into pocket of coat and withdraws the money, which he hands to MENA]* What have you to ate, woman?

[MENA does not answer his question immediately but wraps the notes about the silver coins and transfers the lot to the pocket of her skirt]

Mena: The spuds are boiled. I will make a muller of onion dip. Sit down a tamaill. There is something I have to say to you.

Mike: *[Puzzled]* Yes . . . what?

Mena: Sit here! *[She indicates the chair which he has vacated. He sits on it looking at her expectantly]* It is about Sive.

Mike: Sive!

[MENA sits at the left of the table and places her hands on it]

Mike: What is it about Sive?

Mena: How will I start to tell you? *[Pauses]* There is an account of a match for Sive.

Mike:	*[Screws up his face in wonder]* For Sive? . . . a match? Are you going simple, woman? There is no sense or meaning to you. She's only a child . . . still going to school . . .
Mena:	*[Crossly]* She's old enough! The grass of 20 cows, a farm free of debt; money rotting there.
Mike:	She has no fortune. What farmer of that size would take her without money?
Mena:	He'll be glad to have her, money or no. Think of 20 milch cows and security for the rest of her days.
Mike:	She is different. She has book-learning. She will turn a deaf ear to matchmaking. *[He shakes his head]* I'm her uncle. When my sister died I gave my word that I would stand by her. The girl is too young. She has no father. I have responsibility.
Mena:	Was it your fault, I ask you, that your sister died? Was it your fault that she gave birth to the girl or was too free with men? *[In anger]*
Mike:	*[Warning]* Aisy, a-girl! *[Deadly note]* Aisy! She was young in the ways of the world. She paid dearly for her folly, God help us. She dressed a thorny bed for herself. Will you look how old the world is and how the youth do be so foolish in it.
Mena:	Now listen to me! *[Insistent]* The child was born in want of wedlock. That much is well known from one end of the parish to the other. What is before her when she can put no name on her father? What better can she do when the chance of comfort is calling to her. Will you take stock of yourself, man! There is a fine farm waiting her with servants to tend her so that her hands will be soft and clean when the women of the parish will be up to their eyes in cow-dung and puddle. What better can she do? Who will take her with the slur and the doubt hanging over her?
Mike:	*[Shakes head]* I don't know, woman! I don't know what is best.

Mena: You know as well as I do that what I say is best for the girl.

Mike: Maybe so! . . . Maybe so! . . . *[Puzzled]* But who is the
              man who would marry without a fortune and he having
              that fine bane of cows?

              *[MENA is silent for a moment, looking at him from beneath
              lowered brows]*

Mike: Well?

Mena: *[Pauses, then looks directly at him]* Seán Dóta from the
              foot of the hill.

Mike: *[Open-mouthed, repeating the words slowly]* Seán Dóta!

Mena: *[Hurriedly]* A respectable man with a good bit put away
              by him. And it will mean that we will be rid of your
              mother, too. Sive will take her for company. Wouldn't
              it be wonderful?

              [MIKE suddenly jumps to his feet]

Mike: Never! . . . if the sun, moon and stars rained down out of
              the heavens and split the ground under my feet . . . never!
              'Twill never come to pass while I have the pulse of life in
              me! *[Changes his tone from anger to entreaty]* What devil
              has got into you that you should think of such a thing?
              Even when I was a boy Seán Dóta was a man. The grave
              he should be thinking of. What young girl would look a
              second time at him, a worn, exhausted little lorgadawn of
              a man.

Mena: You are hasty to condemn! Will you sit down and hear me
              out. We will have the house here to ourselves with the
              oul' woman gone as well. *[Suggested note of love]*

Mike: *[Loud voiced]* Never! Not even if the Son of God walked
              the roads of the earth again! She will not darken the door
              of his house.

Mena: Will you sit down, man. You will take flight! Sit here!

Mike: Sit for what . . . ? Sit, is it, to give ear to the greatest
              nonsense within the four walls of the world! You can't be
              in your right mind.

Mena:	There is the gift of £200 for us if there is a marriage. *[Long pause]* Think of the start it would give us. How many times would you bend your back to make it? Long enough we were scraping: you said it yourself. Consider it, will you. It is what we wanted always. Sive will be well off and we will be rid of your mother and her taunting.
Mike:	No! No! A million thousand times no! It would sleep with me for the rest of my days. It would be like tossing the white flower of the canavaun on to the manure heap. It is against the grain of my bones, woman. Will you think of it? Think of what it is! Sive and that oul' corpse of a man, Seán Dóta!
Mena:	*[Soothing motherly tone]* Will you sit down and be said by me.
Mike:	I will not sit! . . . I am going out!
Mena:	*[Repeating his words, her voice filled with sarcasm]* You are going out! *[Changes to a tone of boldness]* Well, if you are going out, I am going with you.
Mike:	*[Lifts his right hand]* There is a finish, girl, to our talk. Leave me to myself. I have a wish to go by myself. Let me be. *[He looks at her, filled with doubt]*
Mena:	*[Pause]* Go away! Go away with you. Go away, man of straw.
Mike:	*[Harshly, loud-voiced]* I am no man of straw. Will you not leave me be with myself?

[Suddenly, in a violent fit of temper, he knocks the chair upon which he has been sitting and goes out, slamming the door. MENA rises and follows him through the door, leaving it open after her, still calling his name.

When both are gone, the old woman comes from the room and looks out after them. She goes to the fire, produces her pipe and lights it. She has only just sat down when a young man enters; aged about nineteen, he is good-looking and manly, his voice cultured and refined. His entrance is somewhat hurried. He is LIAM SCUAB. He carries a few short planks and a bag of tools]

Liam:	I never saw such commotion. First I saw Thomasheen Seán Rua, the matchmaker, sneaking away over the mountain from this house. Next I saw Mike hurrying out of here as if the devil were after him and, last of all I saw Mena running after Mike, calling his name. What's going on at all? Have they all gone mad? *[He puts his tools and planks on table]*
Nanna:	You'd better not be caught here. There will be trouble. Mike Glavin has no liking for you or any of yours, Liam.
Liam:	I wouldn't have called only I was sure there was nobody here but Sive and yourself. I was up the road making a door for Seamus Dónal. Where is she?
Nanna:	*[Archly]* Where is who?
Liam:	*[Smiling]* Come on, you oul' schemer! You know who I mean.
Nanna:	*[Rises and calls to SIVE'S room]* Sive, Liam Scuab is here.
	[SIVE enters]
Sive:	Liam! . . . What brought you?
Liam:	I was passing by; just going the road on business.
Sive:	*[Suddenly alarmed, breaks away]* You'll be caught! *[To NANNA]* Where is Mena . . . my Uncle Mike . . . He'll have a fit, Liam!
Nanna:	Be careful, let ye, and keep a watch. If 'tis a thing ye're caught together there'll be no more peace in this house. *[Exits NANNA]*
Liam:	*[Taking SIVE'S hand]* Will you be able to steal out tonight?
Sive:	If I can, but if I don't come at the time, don't wait.
Liam:	I'll wait till the crack of dawn, anyway.
Sive:	Be careful. Uncle Mike hates you.
Liam:	What harm if he does. He might as well hate me as anybody.
Sive:	*[Pause]* I wonder what Mena and Uncle Mike are doing in the bog?

Liam:	Who knows? I saw Thomasheen Seán Rua, the matchmaker, leaving here too, awhile back.
Sive:	Thomasheen Seán Rua! What did that devil want?
Liam:	Nothing good, I'll warrant. Imagine making a marriage between two people who never saw each other before.
Sive:	Horrible!
Liam:	They say it is necessary in country places.
Sive:	It's horrible, Liam. Would you marry somebody you never saw before?
Liam:	I would marry nobody but you, Sive, I love you. How would I marry anybody but you!
Sive:	*[Pause]* You'd better go. If we're found together . . . !
Liam:	*[Takes his possessions from table]* I'll wait tonight until you come.
Sive:	If I don't come when I say, go home. It's cold and lonely waiting in the dark.
Liam:	It's cold and lonely, too, at home.
Sive:	Look, if I don't come I'll meet you on the road from school tomorrow.
Liam:	Try to come if you can.
	[MIKE enters angrily]
Mike:	What's this? *[louder]* What's this, I say. What are you doing in my house, Liam Scuab? How dare one of your breed cross my door in!
Sive:	*[Timorously]* He was passing by!
Mike:	He was passing by! He was! He was, like a rat when he saw the nest empty. He came stealing and sneaking when we were outside.
Sive:	He was not sneaking and he was not stealing.
Mike:	Go to your room . . . Go on! *[Exit SIVE]*
Liam:	*[Calmly]* No blame to Sive.

Mike: I know your breed, Scuab, and what you are and I know what you're looking for.

Liam: There's no need to sound so dirty about it.

Mike: I know what you're after, Scuab.

Liam: *[Calmly]* I make no denial about it. I'm after Sive.

Mike: I know well what you're after.

Liam: You know one thing and I know another. I say I am after Sive and nothing more that that. I love her.

Mike: Like your snake of a cousin loved her mother mar dhea and fooled her likewise. Like your snake of a cousin that tricked her mother with the promise of marriage and left her a child with no name.

Liam: *[Calmly]* I know who Sive's father is. It is no fault of mine.

Mike: It was the fault of your cousin and ye're the one breed.

Liam: You know as well as I do that he would have married her. You know he went across to England to make a home for her but he was drowned. He never knew she was with child when he left.

Mike: You bring your tale well, don't you? Quick words and book-readin' like all belonging to you. Like your bloody cousin.

Liam: He died, didn't he? What more do you want?

Mike: I want for you to leave here and keep away from Sive. I want that you should never set eyes on her again or you will pay as dear as your cousin paid, maybe.

Liam: You will not command the lives and happiness of two people who love each other.

Mike: *[In a rage]* I will not command . . . the cheek . . . go on, get out of here, you upstart . . . Go on! . . . Go!

Liam: *[Pause. Exiting]* We shall see.

Mike: *[Roaring]* Go on, you tatháire, go on . . .

     [Exit LIAM *waving a hand behind his back in disgust.*

When he has gone MIKE *fumes in the kitchen. After a moment he goes to the door and calls* MENA]

Mike: Mena! . . . Mena! . . .

[MIKE *exits calling her name*]

[*Curtain*]

Scene 2

[*The time: Night; A paraffin lamp burns on a shelf over the fireplace.* SIVE, MIKE *and* MENA *are in the kitchen.*
MIKE *is seated by the fire. In his lap is a pony's collar much worn and patched. With a heavy bent shoemakers needle he stitches a piece of sacking on it.*
SIVE *is seated at the table at end furthest from* MIKE. *Her satchel of books stands open on the table. Her head is bent over a book from which she is memorising sotto voce.*
MENA *stands over the working table, her sleeves rolled up, her back turned to the other two. She is washing a shirt in a tin basin. She takes shirt from basin, squeezes it dry and places it on the table. She takes basin in her hand, goes to door, opens it and throws the dirty water out; closing the door she turns to* MIKE]

Mena: The dogs are barking at the end of the bóithrín. Someone is coming the road.

[MIKE *does not look up from his work.* SIVE *looks abstractedly towards* MENA *and then to her book again.* MENA *places the basin on the working table and pours some water into it from the drinking pail. She takes the shirt and begins to rinse it again in the basin. She turns as though to say something but changes her mind and continues with her washing.* SIVE *closes the book, puts it in bag, takes another. She opens it and continues to memorise part of it.*
There is a knock at the door. MENA *goes to the door and asks*]

Mena: Who is out?

Voice: [*Off, sonorous, high-pitched*] Thomasheen Seán Rua and Seán Dóta from the butt of the hill. Doing a bit of rambling we are.

Mena: Come in, let you!

[The door opens and THOMASHEEN *looks around the kitchen shiftily. He exchanges the barest of glances with* SIVE *who looks at him curiously. He looks cautiously at* MIKE *who ignores him, then at* MENA *who nods to him.* THOMASHEEN *turns and with a motion of his head calls* SEÁN DÓTA. *He enters the kitchen followed by* SEÁN. THOMASHEEN *makes straight for the fire and turns his back to it, lifting his coat-tails to warm himself]*

Thomasheen: *[Shudders]* God save all here. Brr! There is a cold there tonight that would peel the skin from your back. *[To* SEÁN DÓTA, *in a mild pleasing tone]* Come away in from the cold, Seán a chroí. There is a black wind coming around the shoulder of the mountain with fangs in it like the tooth of a boar.

*[*SEÁN DÓTA *advances, shyly, a little ways. He looks for a moment gloatingly at* SIVE, *and smiling shyly looks to* THOMASHEEN.*

      SEÁN is a small man, a little wizened. His age might be anything from 55 to 70. He takes off a bright-coloured cap and holds it supplicatingly in front of him. His hair is whitish-grey worn in a fringe at his forehead. His eyes are birdlike, shrewd. He wears a respectable frieze overcoat which seems too large for him]

Mena: You're welcome here, Seán Dóta. Will you sit up to the fire and let the heat draw the cold out of your bones?

Seán Dóta: No, thanks, Mrs Glavin. I will sit here by the dresser. I'd not like to come in the way of anyone.

[His voice is apologetic. Whenever he speaks he also smiles with a half laugh as if to excuse himself. He sits on a chair by the dresser. He leans forward expectantly with his palms on his knees]

Thomasheen: The heat don't agree with him. He would sooner a cold corner out of the way. *[*SEÁN DÓTA *nods with a half laugh in agreement with* THOMASHEEN*]* He have a very aisy-going manner with him. He have the health of a spring salmon, that man have. You wouldn't like to meet him, he's so nice. *[*SEÁN DÓTA *nods modestly]*

[MIKE holds the collar out at arm's length to examine it. THOMASHEEN watches interestedly]

Thomasheen: You're a great hand for mendin'! There's a drop of the cobbler's blood in your veins, Mike, boy! 'Tis a joy to watch you with the needle. *[MIKE gives him a withering look]*

Mike: *[To MENA]* Maybe they might have mind for a mouthful of tay?

Mena: The kettle is very near the boil.

[SIVE begins to gather her books. Both of the new arrivals protest vigorously at the idea of tea]

Seán Dóta: We're only just after rising from the table. 'Twould be a waste. We're thankful, all the same.

Mena: 'Tis there in plenty if ye have a mind for it.

Thomasheen: Too good you are, woman, to put yourself out for us. *[He goes to the table and stands over SIVE. He looks at the book in front of her. Then to the house at large he says]* Ah, the book-learning is a wonderful thing. Many is the time I have regrets for the idleness of my youth. What a nate curate I would make or a canon maybe, in time with the shoes shining by me night and morning. 'Tis a wise man that puts himself out for the learning. *[To SIVE, cajolingly]* And what is it you have in the book there before you?

Sive: Poetry and verses.

Thomasheen: Ah! *[exhilaratingly]* Poetry. . . . God help us, 'tis far from the poetry book I was reared. There is a verse out of the end of a poem now, I heard a tinker woman reciting back the years. The way it goes . . .

[He cocks his head and purses his lips, then in a stentorian voice almost bawdy in tone, he begins]

'The ripest apple is the soonest rotten;
the hottest love is the soonest cold . . .'

[Out of the corner of his eye he surveys SIVE]

'. . . and a young man's vows, they are soon forgotten;
Go away, young man, do not make so bold!'

[MENA squeezes the shirt, puts it aside, opens the door, and empties the basin]

Mike: *[Politely]* Have you a liking for the versifying, Seán?

Seán Dóta: Divil the bit, Mike. I have nothing against the poets, mind you, but they are filled with roguery and they have the bad tongue on top of it, the thieves. Oh, the scoundrels!

Mena: Have you e'er a poem, Seán? You must have great verses by you, a man with your gentlemanly nature.

Seán Dóta: Oho! *[Deprecatingly, laughs and shakes his head]*

Thomasheen: Ah, he's as deep as a well, woman! As wise as a book! As sharp as a scythe! There's no telling the verses he have.

Mena: Give us a rann out of one of them. I'll bet anything 'tis the best that was ever heard.

[SIVE is amazed at SEÁN's voice and manner. SEÁN looks at her keenly]

Seán Dóta: Begor, then, I will say a verse for the girl. It was from my grandfather I brought it. *[Shifts on his seat]* A very tasty handful of poetry too, it is.

[He coughs, brings his hand to his mouth delicately. In a sing-song voice, very high in tone, he starts]

> 'Seaneen Easter, di-do-dom,
> Stole a pratey from his mom.
> He was caught and he was hung.
> He was buried in the dung.
> When the dung was piking out
> He was hopping like a trout.
> When the dung was piking in
> He was hopping like a hen.'

[MENA acclaims him loudly, as do THOMASHEEN and MIKE. SEÁN shakes his head bashfully, giving the half-laugh again]

Mena: *[Feigning delight]* Well, isn't he the devil's own!

Thomasheen: Ah! he have the humour all over him.

Mike: 'Twas lively, faix!

[MIKE rises, having completed his work on the collar. He places it against the dresser and goes to his seat again]

Mena: Sive, child *[gently]* there's a small journey for you. *[Full of supplication, she comes to where SIVE is sitting. Her manner is pleading, yet considerate]* There's a favour. *[Pause]* Didn't the laths of the rail burst with the weight of turf. Would you by any chance go the road down to the butt of the bóithrín to Seamus Dónal's cottage. Tell him we want the loan of a rail for the morning. He is working in the quarry and sure he'll have no need of it himself. You can tell him it will be called for with the dawn.

Sive: *[Resignedly]* I'll go!

Mena: *[To the house in general]* She's a gift for obliging. *[Her voice is all praise]* She would turn on her heel from whatever she is at, to be of help. *[She helps SIVE on with her coat]*

Sive: *[Reflectively — looking up at MENA childishly]* To be called for at the dawn. I am to tell him the rail was burst with the weight of turf.

Mena: And thank him for the use of it.

[SIVE goes to the dresser for her scarf]

Thomasheen: Well, it's a strange thing that I will be going home by the short cut across the mountain. It was only to keep me company on the road that Seán came as far as this with me. It would be nice for the girl to have his company as far as the foot of the bóithrín. *[Looking around with wide innocent eyes]* And sure 'twould be company for him too. A young heart is a great companion on the road.

Sive: There is no need for Mr Dóta to come with me. I know the road well enough from walking it every day.

Thomasheen: Of course you do, who would know it better? *[Questions the company as if defying contradiction]* But think of the dark, girl, and the púca *[Pauses]* the mad, red eyes of him like coals of fire lighting in his head. There is no telling what you would meet on a black road. There's a mad moon in the sky tonight with the stars out of their mind screeching and roaring at one another.

Seán Dóta: *[Rises from the chair]* I'll be as far as Seamus Dónal's with her. There will no one cross her path with Seán Dóta walking by her side. *[Apologetic laugh]*

Sive: *[Indignantly]* I am not afraid of the dark, or the púca!

Thomasheen: Ah, sure, you would be like a hare on the road with the tidy little white feet of you.

Seán Dóta: It's as well to be going . . . I have the notion of buying a motoring-car *[to impress SIVE]* It is all the fashion these days . . . very saving on the feet. *[Again, the apologetic half-laugh]* By all accounts the women do be driving them, too.

[SEÁN leads the way out, followed by SIVE who looks irritated at the thought of SEÁN's company]

Seán Dóta: Good night all and God bless!

Thomasheen: Good night. God bless.

[THOMASHEEN runs silently to the door, opens it noiselessly and peeps out after them. MENA advances to the fire and stands at one side of it watching THOMASHEEN. MIKE and MENA exchange glances. THOMASHEEN closes door and turns, rubbing hands gleefully]

Thomasheen: The seed is sown; the flower will blossom.

Mena: *[Sits opposite MIKE and faces THOMASHEEN]* The old woman mustn't know . . . the girl will know in good time . . . No need to tell her. It will come over her like a summer tide.

[THOMASHEEN sits facing the fire and runs his fingers through his wild hair, head bent]

Mike: I can't folly with ye! If there was less between them in the years it would be a great day's work. She'll never take with him. It's too much to ask of her.

Mena: Are you forgetting the money? There is a soft bone somewhere in your head, man. And are you forgetting this evening and Liam Scuab.

Mike: I know! I know! the money is a great temptation but there is wrong in it from head to heel. Sive is young, with a brain by her. She will be dreaming about love with a young man. 'Tis the way the young girls do be!

Thomasheen: *[Comes nearer MIKE and extends his hands]* Will you listen to him! Love! In the name of God, what do the likes of us know about love? *[Turns to MENA and points a finger at MIKE]* Did you ever hear the word of love on his lips? Ah, you did not, girl! *[THOMASHEEN rises to the occasion]* Did he ever give you a little rub behind the ear or run his fingers through your hair and tell you that he would swim the Shannon for you? Did he ever sing the love-songs for you in the far-out part of the night when ye do be alone? *[THOMASHEEN scoffs]* He would sooner to stick his snout in a plate of mate and cabbage or to rub the back of a fattening pig than whisper a bit of his fondness for you. Do he run to you when he come in from the bog and put his arms around you and give you a big smohawnach of a kiss and tell you that the length of the day was like the length of a million years while he was separated from you? *[In triumph]* Could you say that he ever brought you the token of a brooch or a bit of finery? . . . Naa! More likely a few pence worth o' musty sweets if the drink made him foolish of a fair day. *[Scornfully]* And to hear you bladderin' about love! The woman would think you were out of your mind if you put a hand around her on the public road. *[MIKE looks hang-dog]*

Mena: You are no one to talk!

Thomasheen: I make no boast either. What I say is what business have the likes of us with love? It is enough to have to find the bite to eat. When I was a young man, 20 years ago, my father, God rest him, put a finish to my bit of love.

Mena: *[In unbelief]* You had love!

Thomasheen: I had a wish for a girl from the other side of the mountain. But what was the good when I had no place to take her. There was a frightful cúram of us in my father's house with nothing but a sciath of spuds on the floor to fill us. I had two pigs fattening. *[Lonesome]* My father was an amadán, a stump of a fool who took his life by his own hand. He hung himself from a tree near the house. I swear to you he would never have hanged himself but he knew my two pigs would pay for his wake and funeral. 'Twas the meanness in his heart, for he knew well I had my heart set on marriage.

Mena: What a lonesome story you have for us.

Thomasheen: Not so lonesome now! There's a widow-woman having a small place beyond the village. £100 would see me settled in with her.

Mike: She will be blessed by you! Will you give her the rub behind the ear? Will you give her brooches and clothes? Ha-ha! I would like to see it!

Thomasheen: Give over! . . . *[To MENA]* There is this young Scuab who have a heart for the girl. He will have fine words for her, looking like a gentleman, with his collar and tie and his poll plastered with hair-*oil*. *[Accent on oil]* I have seen him, after his day's work, looking like a play-actor.

Mena: No fear of him!

Thomasheen: He was in this house this evening!

Mena: You miss nothing!

Thomasheen: You'll have him coming into the house proposin' next! And it might interest you to know that she has been seen on at least one occasion, ducking out of here to meet Scuab after ye were gone to bed.

Mike: This is more serious than I thought and 'twill have to stop! I don't want her going the same road as her mother.

Mena: Then the old woman must know about it and never told us which means she is on their side and is probably even encouraging Sive in this. But there's one easy way to stop that sort of thing and that is to move Sive into the west room where I can keep my eye on her and her only means of coming and going will be through our bedroom.

Thomasheen: But that alone won't be enough! We must cut out every chance of their meeting. Scuab can still meet her and she comin' and goin' to school, so she must finish with her schoolin'. You can say you're no longer able to manage all the work by yourself, that you need her help, else . . .

Mena: There is no fear of him, I tell you!

Mike: You're right, there is no fear of him. He will keep far away from here. But you will have a hard job with Sive.

Thomasheen: Will you listen to him cnáimhseáiling again? He's never happy unless 'tis grumbling he is. Wouldn't you have the good word anyway? You'd swear, to hear you talk, that we were all rogues and thieves.What are we trying to do only make an honest shilling. 'Tisn't going around stealing the dead out of their graves we are. 'Twould be a black day for us if we robbed a widow or stole a poor-box from the chapel. Isn't it only bringing two people together in wedlock we are?

Mena: When will he give the money?

Thomasheen: Seán Dóta is only the half of a fool, not a full one! When the knot is tied and not before. I have the night wasted in talking with ye. The cocks will be crowing by the time I'm home. *[He goes towards door and turns with his hand on latch]* A warning! *[He cocks his thumb towards the old woman's room]* Watch the oul' one up there! She have the makin's of trouble.

[Exist THOMASHEEN SEÁN RUA. MIKE rises, takes a cup from the dresser and goes to tankard. He takes off cover and dips cup, withdrawing it, he drinks with relish]

Mena: I would have made tea for you!

Mike: Tea is scarce enough without wasting it this hour of the night. *[He replaces cup, stretches his hands and yawns. He scratches his head roughly]* I have an early start in the morning and a hard day before me tomorrow. I think I'll go to bed.

Mena: Will you not wait for Sive?

Mike: She will be all right. What can harm her? I have no heart somehow for looking her in the face.

Mena: I think I could sleep myself. *[She arranges fire with tongs while MIKE unlaces and removes his boots]*

Mike: Would my mother have mind, do you think, for tea?

Mena: There is no fear of her! Hasn't she her pipe?

[MENA unlooses her hair, goes to lamp, and lowers wick. She turns and exits by door at side of hearth. MIKE places his boots under the working table and in his socks crosses the kitchen and exits by the same door.

The kitchen is empty, eerie-looking in the bad light.

The door of the old woman's room opens and she enters the kitchen. She tiptoes to the door of the son's room and listens for a moment. Satisfied, she turns away and raises the wick of the lamp. She then sits at her place by the fire. She takes the tongs and re-makes the fire. With a look around her she unearths her pipe and thrusts it into her mouth. She finds matches and lights up. She sits thus for a moment or two.

Suddenly the door opens and SIVE enters. She leans against closed door and holds her hands to her breast, breathing heavily]

Nanna: Where were you until this hour of the night?

Sive: *[Unties her head scarf]* Down the bóithrín at Seamus Dónal's for the loan of a rail for Uncle Mike . . . That old man, Seán Dóta! Oh! *[She shakes her head and covers her face with her hands.]*

Nanna: *[Querulously]* Seán Dóta?

Sive: *[In disgust and fright]* He was on the road down with me. When we passed by the cumar near Dónal's he made a drive at me! He nearly tore the coat off me. I ran into Dónal's kitchen but he made no attempt to follow. Oh, the way he laughs *[in disgust]* like an ould sick thing. What is the meaning of it all, Gran?

Nanna: *[Draws upon her pipe, SIVE sits near her]* 'Tis the nature of the man, child, no more! You will find that men are that way. Being old doesn't change them. It's nothing!

Sive: He frightened the life out of me. I never expected it! *[Pause]* You know, I think, Gran, it was a plan by them . . . but it's so hard to believe.

Nanna: It have the appearance of a plan . . . do you know what I think . . . there are queer doin's goin' on between Mena and Thomasheen Rua.

[MENA emerges from her room wearing a long nightdress reaching to her toes almost. The two start when they see her]

Mena: *[Crossly, loudly]* Are ye going to be there for the night gossiping! A nice thing for the nuns to learn about! Get away to bed out of that! Wasting oil, ye are. Go on! Clear away.

[SIVE and NANNA rise. SIVE hurries to her room. NANNA concealing the pipe in her palm, follows, slowly and casts a defiant look at MENA. Exit NANNA and SIVE. MENA rakes the fire again and quenches lamp altogether]

[Curtain]

SCENE 3

[A week later; late afternoon.

NANNA is at her usual place, MENA is kneading dough to make bread on the large table. A large jug of sour milk and a saucer of flour stand there. MENA lifts the dough and sprinkles flour on the board. She goes to flour bag, refills saucer with flour and returns to the table. She continues with the kneading, dusting the sodden bulk of it at times with flour. She turns her head towards the old woman]

Mena: Is the pot ready?

[NANNA looks at a circular flat-bottomed pot near the fire]

Mena: Is the hearing going by you, on top of everything else? Or is it how you're trying to rise the temper in me?

Nanna: 'Tis aisy enough to do that! The pot is as hot as ever 'twill be.

Mena: And why wouldn't you say so? Sitting there, in the way of everyone!

Nanna: Make your bread, woman! 'Tis hard enough to eat it without having to watch you baking it as well. 'Tis hard enough for a lonely old woman without a child to rock in the cradle.

Mena: Ah, the back o' my hand to you an oul' hag! There is no good in you — alluding and criticising always. Children bring nothing but misfortune. Didn't you see your own — the good end they came to. The gall of you, condemning me for my lack of child.

[MENA kneads the dough vigorously, smooths it in a circle, takes a knife from the cupboard and makes a cross on the top of the loaf. Taking a fist of flour she goes to the hearth and sprinkles the bottom of the pot. She returns to the table, takes the dough in her hands and places it in the pot. She takes the tongs and pushing the pot nearer the fire, arranges coals around it. She takes a cloth from the cupboard and cleans the table]

Mena: Keep an eye to the bread. I'm going out to give hay to the cows.

Nanna: *[Pointedly]* Are you sure it is the cows you are going to see? Are you sure it isn't making mischief you're going?

Mena: *[Crossly]* What is behind that?

Nanna: Well enough you know what is behind it.

Mena: Come out with what you have to say. Don't be going around in circles like a salmon in a pool.

Nanna: Fine words!

Mena: Is it how you're twisted inside of you that you must have the double meaning the whole time?

Nanna: I will have what meaning I like! God gave me my tongue, not you!

Mena: Not when you are meaning me, will you have strange meanings. What is behind your words?

Nanna: That the heart might wither up in your breast — you know what is behind my words. What is the secrecy between yourself and Thomasheen Seán Rua? What is bringing the old man, Seán Dóta, here, day in day out? Will you have the gall to answer?

Mena: *[Indignant]* What has it to do with you?

Nanna: It is my grand-daughter that is concerned.

Mena: *[Throws back her head and scoffs]* Your grand-daughter . . . and do you know, old woman, who her father is? Maybe you will tell? Thanking me from her heart, she should be, the fine match I am making for her. Putting myself out to place her in a gentleman's house.

Nanna:	Suiting yourself you are, like you always did.
Mena:	*[Viciously]* Go to hell!

[There is a knock on the door]

Mena:	Come in. let you!

[Enter THOMASHEEN SEÁN RUA. He gives the customary furtive glance around the kitchen, his eyes coming to rest on the old woman. MENA nods encouragingly to him and he advances, leaving door open behind him]

Nanna:	Was there no door in the last house you were in?
Thomasheen:	*[Carrying an ashplant, hoists it dexterously in his hand]* The deaf ear is the only cure for your equals . . . *[Then, to MENA]* You will have company shortly, I am thinking.

[Goes to door, looks out to his right and turns again]

Mena:	Who is on the road?
Thomasheen:	Father and son but brothers likewise since the pair of them are sons of the devil.
Mena:	Who is that?
Thomasheen:	Two tinker-men . . . Pats Bocock and his son Carthalawn. Two robbers who have no liking for me or any of mine.
Nanna:	Dacent poor people with no home of their own. Good friends when they are needed.
Thomasheen:	You know your own! But I know them as rogues! They would cut my gad because I have great call at the match-making.
Nanna:	I would be proud to own them. *[Eyes MENA coldly]* They are visiting here with many a year.
Mena:	With the hands out and the mouths open, by them. Nothing more and nothing less than beggars.
Nanna:	They are the people of the road — travelling people. They are above the class beggar.

[In the distance is the sound of a bodhrán and a voice singing. The sound increases while the occupants of the

*kitchen await PATS BOCOCK and CARTHALAWN. The air of
the song is that of "Neath the Bright Silvery Light of the
Moon' — the Irish ballad not to be confused with 'By the
Light of the Silvery Moon', the American ballad. The words
of the song are impromptu and created by CARTHALAWN]*

**[N.B. — the same air will persist in all his songs
throughout the remainder of the play]**

*[Enter CARTHALAWN and PATS BOCOCK. They keep step with
each other. PATS is dressed in an ancient swallow-tail coat
and ancient trousers with strong boots. His hat is normal
but the hollow in the crown is pushed upwards to give it
the gaudy appearance of a top hat. He carries a stout
blackthorn stick which he taps on the floor with each step.
His left leg is shorter than his right and he walks with a
lop-sided motion. He is of stern appearance but looks
poverty-stricken nevertheless.*

*His son, CARTHALAWN, wears a short coat and is otherwise
dressed as his father. In short, his dress is typical of the
southern tinker who never wears a collar and tie, who has
a jaunty air of good health about him but is above all hard
of face. He carries a small bodhrán.*

*What is important about the pair is that both of them
keep the same step like soldiers on the march and have
an understanding between each other.*

*Entering the kitchen both men come to a halt before
the large table. PATS strikes the floor with his stick and
taking up the rhythm CARTHALAWN taps the bodhrán with
his knuckles.*

*He strikes loudly at first, then gently with a very low
rubbing of knuckles, preparatory to singing.*

*NANNA rises to her feet, as is the custom when travelling
minstrels enter a house because the first song must be in
praise of the man of the house who is generally absent at
work in the fields.*

*As the sound of the bodhrán decreases, the tapping of
PATS' stick becomes stronger. Then suddenly the tapping of
stick and sound of bodhrán become extremely faint and
CARTHALAWN begins his song. His voice is bell-like in tone.
The accent is slightly nasal]*

Carthalawn: *[Singing]*   Oh! Mike Glavin, you're the man;
You was always in the van;
With a dacent house to old man and
    gorsoon;
May white snuff be at your wake,
Bakers bread and curran-y cake
And plinty on your table, late and soon.

[NANNA applauds the song, while MENA and THOMASHEEN are indifferent. PATS advances and shakes hands with NANNA]

Pats: *[Deep-voiced and solemn with unsmiling face]* 'Tis not aisy, a-girl, to kill you! You have the appearance of a small one, a young one. We do be praying for you in our prayers, whenever we get the notion to kneel. *[He turns to MENA]* God bless you, bean an tí with your fine appearance and your name for generosity.

[PATS shakes hands with MENA. Her reaction is dismal and suspicious. PATS ignores her indifference and extends his hand to THOMASHEEN who turns his back to PATS]

Nanna: *[In a loud voice, full of warning]* You are as well off, Pats, without the paw of the devil burning your palm.

[PATS returns to his son's side; both stand rigid]

Mena: What is it ye want?

Pats: No more than a dorn of sugar and a dusteen of tea. We have the caravan beyant in the steamrolled road. Liam Scuab *[He bends his head in thanks while CARTHALAWN stands rigid]* a dacent man, gave us the side of a loaf. We have our own accoutrements. If there is the giving of tea and sugar we will thank the hand that gives it. If there is not, maybe there is the giving of a silver piece. Is there anything from Thomasheen Seán Rua of the mountain — making it in plenty he is.

[PATS extends his palm to THOMASHEEN who has turned again to face him]

Thomasheen: *[Slightly panicky]* Where would the likes of me come by silver money? There is the half of the county looking for men to work in the bogs. Why should a man beg when there is work before and after him?

Nanna: There is no luck in refusing a man of the road!

[PATS looks with hard eyes at THOMASHEEN, who surveys him with superiority, both hands held behind his back. PATS opens his mouth and throws back his head in a dangerous fashion. Tapping his stick on the floor, he makes a circuit of the table to where CARTHALAWN stands. He stands by his son's side still tapping]

Pats: Carthalawn!
[CARTHALAWN turns towards his father, a wild look in his eyes]
Your best! Your mighty best!

[Violently PATS begins to tap his stick upon the floor. CARTHALAWN looks upward at the ceiling and begins to tap the bodhrán with clenched knuckles. For a moment there is loud timing of stickbeat and bodhrán. Then the sound dwindles and CARTHALAWN takes up the beat to his usual air, while the stick is pointed at THOMASHEEN]

Carthalawn: *[Still at 'attention', addresses himself to THOMASHEEN while his father stands at 'attention']*

> May the snails devour his corpse,
> And the rain do harm worse;
> May the devil sweep the hairy crature soon;
> He's as greedy as a sow;
> As the crow behind the plough;
> That black man from the mountain, Seánín Rua!

[PATS stamps both his legs and his stick with delight, NANNA crows with aged laughter. THOMASHEEN turns his back again, boiling with impotent rage. CARTHALAWN, having fulfilled his duty, stands unsmiling]

Nanna: I will give ye the grain o' tay and sugar out of respect to yeer singing.

[MENA immediately goes and takes her stand between NANNA and the dresser]

Mena: *[Like a guard at arms]* You will give nothing! Is it how you think that tea and sugar are made by wishing?

Thomasheen: *[Turning around viciously]* Arrah, that's right! Give nothin'!
[Pronounced 'Notten'] Give nothin'!! *[He cranes his neck
forward]* The smart men o' the roads. Goin' around criticisin'
dacent men an' women. *[THOMASHEEN advances a step,
assured of MENA's help]* Tea and sugar, how are you? the
cheek of the two biggest robbers walking the roads of
Ireland.

*[PATS and CARTHALAWN back towards the door, fearful of
their ground. THOMASHEEN, thinking he has gained the
ascendancy, follows up his victory. PATS and CARTHALAWN
stand in line with the door]*

Thomasheen: *[Confident]* Will ye look at the appearance of them! A short
leg and a half-fool! Two with the one word, goin' around
with their songs, frightenin' half the country. Go on away
to yeer smelly caravan and not be disgustin' respectable
people!

*[THOMASHEEN draws back his right hand as if to strike them.
As he does so, PATS taps again with his stick. CARTHALAWN
knuckles the bodhrán. Both assume ritual dignity to the
rhythm of bodhrán and blackthorn]*

Pats: *[To CARTHALAWN]* Carthalawn, your best! Your Almighty best!
*[With temper he keeps tapping. Imperiously he points stick
at THOMASHEEN as in a ritual from time immemorial.
CARTHALAWN sings slowly, his voice bell-like and piercing.
The tapping and the bodhrán grow quieter]*

Carthalawn: *[Sings]*   On the road from Abbeyfeale,
Sure I met a man with meal,
Come here, said he, and pass your idle time;
On me he made quite bold
Saying the young will wed the old
And the old man have the money for the child.

*[THOMASHEEN turns to look to MENA who stands helpless. PATS
taps his stick loudly on the floor with appreciation, full of
smiles and headshaking. NANNA crows with delight
simultaneously. THOMASHEEN returns to where MENA stands
barring NANNA's way to the dresser. MENA folding her hands
over her bosom in a fighting attitude, advances until she
faces CARTHALAWN and his father]*

Mena: You brought your story well! *[To PATS]* Come out with what you have to say. Don't be hiding behind the words of a half-fool. *[Indicating CARTHALAWN]*

Pats: 'Tis the talk of the country that Seán Dóta the farmer is marrying a young girl out of this house. If their tales are true her name is Sive. The people are saying that it is a strange match that a young girl who is at the start of her days should marry an old man who is at the end of his. They say he is struggling to keep the spark of life inside of him. They say she is the flower of the parish.

Mena: How dare you cast your aspersions under this roof.

Pats: *[Calmly]* 'Tis only what the people are saying! *[He points his stick at THOMASHEEN]* They say he is the man who brought it about; that he will score well out of it. 'Tis only what the people are saying. *[Roguishly]* What is the common word everywhere our feet take us.

Mena: And what is it to them or to you either, the way we conduct ourselves? Is it the first time a young girl married a man older than her? She is matching well for herself.

Pats: There is no one saying otherwise.

Nanna: The devil's work, that's what it is!

Pats: We will come calling the night of the wedding.

Thomasheen: There will be nothing here for ye.

Pats: We will come all the same, welcome or not!

Nanna: There was always welcome here for Pats Bocock.

Pats: 'Tis the changing of the times.

Thomasheen: *[To PATS]* 'Twill be a good change when the likes of ye do a day's work. Into jail ye should be put, a brace of dirty beggars.

Pats: *[Full of venom]* I'm listening to you, Thomasheen Seán Rua and I'm watching you and I'm telling you what you are. You are the bladder of a pig, the snout of a sow; you are the leavings of a hound, the sting of a wasp. You will die roaring. Carthalawn! your best! Your almighty best!

[PATS stands rigid and taps the stick. CARTHALAWN knuckles bodhrán, volume is reduced and CARTHALAWN sings as both men turn for the door in step]

Carthalawn: *[Singing]*   May the snails devour his corpse
And the rains do harm worse
May the devil sweep the hairy creature soon;

[They go out, but the singing is heard, growing fainter]

He's as greedy as a sow,
As the crow behind the plough,
That black man from the mountain, Seánín Rua.

[THOMASHEEN goes to the door and closes it after PATS and CARTHALAWN. Flexing the stick with his hands behind his back, he glares at NANNA]

Thomasheen: Who has been broadcasting my private affairs around the countryside. *[With NANNA alone he is confident again and bent upon cowarding her]* You are a lone woman with your husband feeding worms in his trench. You have terrible gumption with no one left to back you.

Mena: Go on, you oul' wretch . . . Answer the man . . . Where is your stiffness gone to?

Thomasheen: With the county home staring you in the face?

Mena: Dependent upon people who work and scrape to make ends meet.

Nanna: Ye had . . .

Thomasheen: Go on! Say it, you oul' hag! Aaaah! You'll say nothin' now. Face the end of your days, oul' woman!

Nanna: Ye had little to say a while back, either of ye, when the composing was going on. I will tell my son when he comes home the way ye are at me.

Mena: Little your son cares about you. Long ago you should have been put in your place. Small thanks you show for the freedom you have here. Would it not enter your head that there is many an oul' woman of your age walking the road without a roof above or a bed beneath them.

Thomasheen: Sure the county home is filled to the jaws with the likes of her. You will see the crowds of them sticking their heads out of the windows watching the visitors coming and going and they hoping that someone will come to take them away out of it. 'Tis the sport of Cork to see the way they do be haggling and scraping over the few potatoes and the forkful of meat. *[Solemnly]* Ah, but sure the hardest of all, God pity us, is that they will stop the oul' women of smoking. An oul' lady from the other side of the mountain that used to have a liking for her pipe of tobaccy went out of her mind after three days. She could be heard screeching in the other world. They had a piece of sacking over her mouth to keep her quiet but sure that was no good but as little. She started scraping herself till the flesh hung from her in gibbles and the blood used to be coursin' down out of her in streams. 'Twas a madness for the pipe, you see! *[Sanctimoniously]* She was a terrible sight when she died. They buried her in the middle of the night with not a living Christian in the world of her own people to say a prayer for her . . . Aaah! Some people do not know when they are well off!

Mena: She will change!

Thomasheen: She have the appearance of a one that won't!

Mena: She'll change! She's enough of a burden without becoming a curse altogether.

Thomasheen: Walking the road she should be like the rest of her equals.

Mena: Will she walk the road? . . . Far from it . . . Where is the independent woman we had in her? *[MENA lifts latch and opens doors. She indicates the world beyond with a flourish]* Go on, if you have the mind for it! *[Shouts]* Go on and put your bag on your back and go begging from door to door. Will she go, do you think? . . . will she? . . . No! nor go! What a fool she would be to leave her warm fire with the pipe handy by her and the good table with her three rounds of diet every day.

Nanna: *[To the fire]* There is a hatchery of sin in this house *[Her voice is full of defeat. MENA bounces forward till she is close to NANNA. THOMASHEEN advances likewise]*

Mena: *[Violently]* No more of your sharp answers, you oul' wretch. You sit there, day in, day out, taking all you can get without a word of thanks. You will have a puss by you like the child in the cot feeding yourself up with the fruits of our labours, taking all as if you were born for it, like the queen of the land.

Nanna: *[Repeats]* 'Like a child in the cradle'. *[Shakes her head pitifully]*

Mena: *[Stiffens with rage]* Is it my fault that your son is a tired gomaral of a man?

Nanna: A cluckin' hen won't hatch!

Mena: *[Advances and draws back her hand]* I will strike you. *[Full of venom]* I will take the head from your shoulders.

[MENA draws back her hand again to strike a blow. THOMASHEEN drops his stick, intervenes promptly, and drags MENA back towards the door, she struggles in his grasp, to have at NANNA, but he holds her firmly]

Thomasheen: *[From behind MENA, still holding her, to NANNA]* See what you're after doing? *[Guilefully]* You have her upset. *[To NANNA]* You will answer for your evil soul.

Mena: She'll burn! She'll burn the day she gives over life!

Thomasheen: *[To NANNA]* Don't be goadin' her! Don't be goadin' her.

Nanna: *[Having crossed to her bedroom door, NANNA turns]* I'll say it again. There's a hatchery of sin in this house.

[When she has gone, THOMASHEEN releases his hold on MENA who looks with murderous intent towards the room into which NANNA has entered]

Thomasheen: Leave her be for the now. The mind for fight is gone from her. *[He stoops, and retrieves his stick, and makes small circles on the floor with its point]* There is a play to all things. D'you see th' oul' cock salmon that do be hidin' in the deep hole in the river. They will be firing stones at him and making plans for his capture. They will be poisoning and making the use of nets but they might as well be idle. *[Is very positive]* 'Tis the age that will do the work. 'Tis the mounting up of the years. Aaah! age is a killin' thief! Age is

the boy that will stand no nonsense. He have a grip like
a double-knot . . . The old woman is tiring.

[Pause]

Mena: When will he give the money?

Thomasheen: If there is a wedding, 'twill be on the morning of the
wedding, on the word of a man. Is there any word out
of the girl.

Mena: She will do what is to be done. Am I to be telling you
forever?

Thomasheen: But have she said the word out of her mouth?

Mena: What is the need for that?

Thomasheen: It would put my mind more at ease.

Mena: Well, you can rest your mind. She will marry Seán Dóta
and that will be the end of it.

Thomasheen: 'Tis a fine thing to hear the good word anyway. Still I may
tell you I will not rest happy till he have the halter on her.

Mena: *[Raises a hand to* THOMASHEEN *to ensure silence — she
listens a moment]* That will be Sive now. When she comes
in, pass her the time of day — no more; then go away
about your business and leave the rest in my hands.
'Tis work for a woman now.

Thomasheen: *[Hurries to window and looks out]* You will put the best
things before her.

Mena: Gather yourself and be ready to go.

Thomasheen: What about? . . . *[He points to* NANNA'S *room]*

Mena: She'll dance to my tune . . . Aisy!

[The latch lifts and SIVE *enters. She is dressed as before and
carries the satchel of books in her hand. She looks from*
MENA *to* THOMASHEEN, *frowns for the barest fraction of a
second and lays her satchel on the table. She undoes
her headscarf and lays it across the satchel]*

Thomasheen: *[Sweetly]* Is the schoolin' over for today with ye?

Sive: *[To MENA]* The bicycle got punctured again. I had to walk from beyond the cross.

Thomasheen: I will have to be going. There is a great length coming to the days, thanks be to God. We will have the summer now down on the door before we know it.

Mena: Good-bye to you, Thomasheen.

Thomasheen: *[Nods politely to SIVE, who edges away to let him pass]* I will be seeing ye again, please God, before we're older.

Mena: *[Impatiently]* We will be here! *[Inclination of head]*

[THOMASHEEN twirls his stick and opens the door]

Thomasheen: *[Airily]* Good luck, all.

[When he has gone, MENA takes one of the buckets from under the working table and pours water from the drinking pail into it. She replaces the drinking pail. MENA then scoops several fistfuls of meal from the bag into the bucket]

Sive: *[Hesitant]* The tubes of the bicycle are full of holes.

[MENA dries her hands on her apron and turns to SIVE]

Mena: *[Sympathetically]* We will have to do something about it, for sure. I will tell himself to be on the lookout for a pair of new tubes in the village. Will I wet a mouthful o' tea for you while you're waiting for the dinner. *[SIVE is too surprised to reply]* There is a piece of sweet cake I have put away. You must be tired after your day.

Sive: *[Befuddled]* No . . . no . . . don't bother with the tea! I'll wait until the dinner.

Mena: A cup of milk, so! *[Without waiting for reply, she hurries to dresser, takes a cup, fills it and forces it on SIVE]* It must be an ease for you to get away from the nuns and the books but sure we won't have much more of schooling now.

[Gently MENA forces SIVE to a chair near the table. SIVE places the cup before her and looks bewilderedly at MENA at the word 'school']

Mena: Any of the girls in the parish would give their right hand to have the chance that's before you.

Sive: But . . .

Mena: *[Quickly before SIVE can reply]* Don't think about it now. Think of the handling of thousands and the fine clothes and perfumery. Think of the hundreds of pounds of creamery cheques that will come in the door to you and the servant boy and the servant girl falling over you for fear you might dirty your hands with work.

Sive: *[Shakes her head several times as though to ward off MENA's words]* You don't know . . . you . . . you . . .

Mena: Sit down now and rest yourself. You could have your grandmother with you. Think of the joy it would give the poor woman to have the run of such a fine house . . . and to see you settled there. 'Tis a fine thing for you my girl and sure, what matter if he's a few years older than you. Won't we be all old in a handful of short years? Ah! I would give my right hand to be in your shoes.

Sive: *[Shakes her head continually]* Please, please . . . you don't know what you are saying. How can you ask me such a thing?

Mena: Now, tomorrow himself will call to the convent and tell the reverend mother that you will not be going in any more. What would a grown-up woman like you want spending your days in the middle of children.

Sive: I could never live with that old man. *[Entreats MENA]* Fancy the thought of waking in the light of day and looking at him with the small head of him. Oh, my God! No! I could never! . . . I could not even think of it!

Mena: *[Still motherly]* Nonsense, child! That is nothing. Have sense for yourself. I know what you are going into. Do you think I would not gainsay him if it wasn't the best thing for you. *[Places a hand around SIVE's shoulder]* Sit here, child, and drink your milk.

[MENA gently brings SIVE to the chair, seats her and stands behind her with both hands resting lightly on SIVE's shoulders. MENA's face becomes shrewd. SIVE looks vacantly before her — towards the audience]

Mena: Will you picture yourself off to the chapel every Sunday
in your motor-car with your head in the air and you giving
an odd look out of the window at the poor óinsheacs in
their donkey-and-cars and their dirty oul' shawls and their
faces yellow with the dirt by them. Will you thank God that
you won't be for the rest of your days working for the bare
bite and sup like the poor women of these parts.

Sive: *[Raises her head and entwines her hands]* Imagine what
the girls at school would say! Imagine going to a dance
with him, or going up the chapel with him!

Mena: All I know is that you will be independent. You will have
no enemy when you have the name of money.

Sive: I don't know what to think or to say. I do not want to give
offence but I will never marry such a man. I will not marry
at all!

Mena: *[Motherly again]* You will change! You will change when
you think by yourself of the misery you are leaving; when
you think of the way you were born.

        *[SIVE eagerly turns and looks innocently at MENA. She is
        changed suddenly to an eager girl awaiting the solution
        of a problem that has for a long time baffled her]*

Sive: Surely you don't remember when I was born. *[Her eyes
widen as she looks at MENA. For the first time she takes an
interest in MENA's soliloquy]* Nobody ever told me about
my father or mother or what sort of people they were.

        [SIVE looks into MENA's face searching for the truth]

Mena: I will tell the tale. Himself would never bring himself to
say it. You would think it was some kind of a blemish that
should be hidden and sure, what was it, only the work of
nature. Your mother, God grant her a bed in heaven, was
a nice lie of a girl. Your father took himself away quickly
out of these parts and, if he is alive, never made himself
known. There was no blame to your mother, God help her.
Your grandmother, for all yeer talking and whispering
behind my back, was never the one to come out with the
truth.

Sive: But my father . . . wasn't he drowned in England?

Mena: Your father was never a father, God forgive him. He
                     straightened his sails and disappeared like the mist of a
                     May morning. It was no wonder your mother died with
                     the shame of it. No blame, a chroí! *[With feeling then]*
                     No blame to what is mortal. Do you think it is how two
                     people will stay apart forever who have blood becoming
                     a flood in their veins. It is the way things happen . . .
                     [conviction] . . . the sound of fiddles playing airy hornpipes,
                     the light of a moon on the pale face of a river, the whispered
                     word . . . the meeting of soft arms and strong arms . . .
                     [Pauses] . . .

Sive: I thought you said you'd tell me about my father.

Mena: *[Unaccountably vexed]* I'm telling you your father was
                     nothing. He was no father. He had no name. You have no
                     name. You will have no name till you take a husband. Do
                     you see the hungry greyhound or the mongrel dog? It is the
                     same way with a man. It is no more than the hunger. It is
                     time you were told, my girl. You are a bye-child, a common
                     bye-child — a bastard!

                     *[SIVE attempts to rise. MENA roughly pushes her back in her
                     chair]*

Mena: You will sleep with that old woman no longer. *[She flings
                     the schoolbag across the room]* There will be no more
                     school for you. School is a place for schoolmasters and
                     children. Every woman will come to the age when she
                     will have a mind for a room of her own. I mind when I
                     was a child, *when I was a woman*, there were four sisters
                     of us in the one room. There was no corner of a bed we
                     could call our own. We used to sit into the night talking
                     and thieving and wondering where the next ha'penny
                     would come from or thinking would it ever come to our
                     turn to meet a boy that we might go with, and be talking
                     with and maybe make a husband out of. We would kill.
                     [Vexed] We would beg, borrow or steal. We would fire
                     embers of fire at the devil to leave the misery of our own
                     house behind us, to make a home with a man, any man
                     that would show four walls to us for his time in the world.

[In a voice of warning] Take no note of the man who has nothing to show for himself, who will be full of raiméis and blather, who would put wings on ould cows for you but has no place to make a marriage bed for you. Take heed of a man with a piece of property. He will stand over his promise. He will keep the good word to you because he has the keeping of words . . . Now go to the room and be sure to think of what I said.

[SIVE rises instinctively goes towards her own room but remembering, turns and exits by the far door to MENA's bedroom]

[End of Act One]

ACT TWO

Scene 1

[MENA sits at the table preparing the shopping list for the wedding. There is a knock on the door]

Mena: *[Listens a moment]* Come in!

[Enter LIAM SCUAB. He looks around the kitchen]

Mena: You have the devil's own gall coming here. Lucky for you that Mike is away.

Liam: I don't give a hatful of bornacks for Mike or for your either. I come here to see Sive.

Mena: What do you want Sive for?

Liam: I want to talk with her.

Mena: You put a journey on yourself for nothing. Sive isn't here. *[Turning away to re-arrange fire]*

Liam: How is it her bike is up against the wall of the house?

Mena: *[Angry]* Are you telling me she's here? Are you making a liar out of me in my own house?

Liam: I didn't call you a liar. I only thought you might be making a mistake.

Mena: *[Loudly]* Same thing, isn't it? Didn't I say she wasn't here?

Liam: There's no harm if I wait for her so. I won't be in the way.

Mena: You have no business here. If Mike finds you there will be war. You're not wanted in this house. Clear off on your road and don't be vexing me.

Liam: I have no wish to make an enemy out of you. I will wait till she comes.

Mena: *[Violently]* Will you have your own way in all things, will you? Will you be coming into people's houses causing trouble. Get away out of here or I'll get the tongs to you.

Liam: I love her!

Mena:	*[Mimicking]* You love her! You do! You love her! You gomaral.
	[There is a sound without, and MIKE enters]
Mena:	Look, what's before you! Look at him and don't blame me because he wouldn't go for me.
Mike:	*[In overcoat with cap, places sack and whip aside and throws cap on table]* I see him! *[MIKE sits on the sack]*
Liam:	I mean no harm, Mike Glavin, to you or your wife.
Mike:	*[Taking off his boots]* What do you want Scuab?
Liam:	I want to see Sive.
Mike:	*[Mutters thoughtfully]* You came to see Sive, did you? Sive, faith, of all ones! What do you want to see her for, Scuab?
Liam:	To have a talk with her.
Mike:	*[Calmly]* No, you'll have no talk with her.
Liam:	Only for a moment.
Mike:	She's in my care. You'll have to talk with me.
Liam:	I know you won't heed me but I was told that Sive was getting married.
Mike:	Who told you that?
Liam:	The two tinkers, Carthalawn and Pats Bocock. They were singing a song. It was easy to read the news.
Mena:	Now for sure you're a fool, when you pay attention to the grunting of pigs.
Liam:	They make sense in their own way.
Mike:	'Tis nonsense.
Liam:	If it is nonsense, so, tell me why is Thomasheen Seán Rua, the matchmaker, coming here every day and often twice in the day?
Mike:	He has his own business with me. You're like a magistrate with your foxy digs at us.

Liam: All right, so, but what is the reason for another thing?

Mike: What other thing?

Liam: The old man, Seán Dóta, the farmer; he is coming here every day now too.

Mike: Is he now, and what do you make out of it all?

Liam: I have heard him talking to himself on the road.

Mena: Talking to himself, will you tell us?

Liam: I have heard him.

Mena: And what does he be saying?

Liam: Things about Sive, and how he will warm her before she is much older. A lot of other things, too, but most of it not fit to mention again.

Mike: *[Crossly]* So what if he does? What is it to you?

Liam: I know he will marry Sive.

[MIKE and MENA exchange shrewd looks]

Mike: Ah, yerra, you're going farther from sense with every word.

Mena: Sure, isn't that what I told him.

Liam: It's hard to believe it could be true.

Mike: There is no truth at all to it, man.

Liam: Oh, for God's sake, will the two of you stop treating me like a child. The whole parish knows what's going on. It is the talk at every crossroads that Sive is matchmaking with Seán Dóta. In the village the public-houses are full with the mockery of it.

Mike: *[Advancing a step]* I've come to the last sod with you, Scuab. Get out of this house before I be tempted to take a weapon in my hands. *[Clenches fists]* You'd better be going, Scuab, or I'll take the whip to you.

Mena: And I the tongs. I'll put streaks on you worse than a raddle-stick.

Liam:	*[Pleads]* In the honour of God, I beseech you to forget about violence. I tell you I want no trouble. If I have upset ye, I'm sorry, but surely if ye know God ye must think of this terrible auction. Ye must know that a day will dawn for all of us when an account must be given. Do not think of me. I promise I will leave these parts till Sive is a woman. I swear that on my dead mother. But do not give her to that rotting old man with his gloating eyes and trembling hands.
Mike:	*[Less angrily]* Enough, Scuab! Go! *[Turns aside]*
Mena:	Wasn't it one of your breed that blackened her mother's name, wasn't it? Oh, the cheek of you, you upstart out of the gutter.
Liam:	Think, woman, I beg of you! Think, Mike Glavin! Forget about yourselves and see it with good eyes instead of greedy ones. Have you knowledge of the Crucified Son of God? *[Shakes his head with emotion]* Are you forgetting Him who died on Calvary? Are you forgetting the sorrow and terrible sadness of His Bloody Face as He looks at ye now? Will ye stand and watch each other draw the hard crooked thorns deep into His helpless body?
Mena:	*[Violent temper]* Gerraway out-a that! Get away!
Liam:	*[Backing towards door]* Nothing in Heaven or Hell could move ye to see wrong!
	[MENA whips the sharp knife off the dresser]
Mena:	I'll open you! I'll open you if you vex me more.
Liam:	I'm going. You'll live to remember this night.
	[Exit LIAM. MENA scowlingly replaces knife and looks at MIKE who stands sullen]
Mena:	What's wrong with you now?
Mike:	Nothing!
Mena:	Well, put a stir on yourself. You have a priest to see.
Mike:	*[Sighs]* Aye!
	[Enter SIVE looking a little wan]

Sive: I thought I heard the voice of Liam Scuab.

Mena: You thought right! He was here.

Sive: What was he looking for?

Mena: He's a strange one! He came wishing you joy. You'd never think he would. He wished you joy and plenty on your wedding.

Sive: *[In astonishment]* He wished me joy and plenty!

Mena: *[Nods]* And he'll pray for your happiness and he's going away altogether to foreign places. That is the last we'll see of him, God help us. That the blessing of God go with him!

Sive: *[In wonder]* Did he say any more?

Mena: *[To MIKE]* Did he say any more?

Mike: Mmmmm!

Mena: Divil the word more, only to turn on his heel as airy as you please and off with him.

Sive: He's gone for good? *[Turns towards room]* To think that he's gone for good.

Mena: Gone, he is!

Sive: *[Tearfully]* Oh! Liam could never do a thing like that.

               [She turns with her hands to her face and exits]

Mena: There 'tis all now settled and no more to it.

Mike: She has no heart for it.

Mena: She'll have heart in time. 'Twill be nothing at all when she gets settled in for herself. What way was I when I came to this house? No one to say a good word for me and amn't I coming into my own now in spite of all?

Mike: That was a different story! You were wanting to get married. Sive has no wish for it.

Mena: *[Crossly]* Are you at it again? Cnáimhseáiling! It was different in no way. How was it different? With an oul' devil in the corner screechin' at me the length of the day and a dirty brat of an orphan bawling in the corner.

Mike:	Sive is young!
Mena:	*[Indignantly]* And wasn't I young?
Mike:	I know! I know! But . . .
Mena:	But this, and but that! I'm going for a bucket of water to the well. You can eat, if you want it.
Mike:	I'll shave if I'm to see the priest.
Mena:	*[Taking the bucket]* There's water in the kettle for you.
	[Exit MENA]
Mike:	I can eat a bit when I'm done.

[MIKE takes brush, soap and an open razor and places them on working table. He fetches kettle and pours water into basin on table, finds towel in cupboard and sets about softening his bristle.

Enter NANNA silently. She is on her way to her chair by the fire when her movement is arrested by a sudden thought. She turns]

Nanna:	What are you shaving for at this hour of the day? Is it Sunday or Monday we have?
Mike:	*[Without turning]* Is it a sin to shave? Must I answer for everything?
Nanna:	*[Tone of menace]* You will answer for enough in your own time.

[MIKE spins around suddenly, holding soap and brush in hands]

Mike:	And what is this, all of a sudden?
Nanna:	There is a curse of evil on this house. Your dead sister and my dead daughter will curse it from her grave.
Mike:	*[Wearily, irritably]* Will ye never stop pestering me?
Nanna:	There was never an ounce of luck in this house since that greasy bitch darkened the door of it.
Mike:	*[Dangerously]* You mean, who?

Nanna:	I mean that hungry sow that sleeps with you. I mean that pauperised wretch you call a wife.
Mike:	You never had a good word for her. She's my wife and she'll always be that. A man's wife will always be his wife, let them both be what they will.
Nanna:	Far be it from me to spoil your home and put ye fighting. But surely you must give an ear to the word of your own mother that suckled you when you were a tiny boy, that watched over you like a hawk, that kept the wind and the rain away from you. *[Near to tears]* Surely you will listen to your own mother that loved you as no one ever will.
Mike:	*[Weary, considerate]* What ails you, mother . . . what ails my mother?
Nanna:	Sive, Mike, Sive! Poor Sive! What are ye doing to her? Is there no heart in you at all?
Mike:	*[Head averted]* 'Tis for the best, I tell you. 'Tis for the best.
Nanna:	'Tis for the best that she marry an ould fooleen of a man! Mike, you will not look at me in the face and say 'tis for the best! Will you look at me in the face, my son!
Mike:	Are you trying to drive nails into me? What am I to do? Do you want to have *she* be like her poor mother? Don't you know that Scuab has an eye for her?
Nanna:	Liam Scuab is a good boy. He would make a good husband. There is lies to you, Mike!
Mike:	Did his cousin make a good husband for Sive's mother? Will you have her conceiving again under sin? Will you have another Scuab do bad work?
Nanna:	That is a wrong thing to say, leanbh! Oh! 'tis a wrong thing. Sive and Liam Scuab will not wear under temptation. There is a sweet thing in their love. Shame to you, Mike!
Mike:	Will you forget so quick? Quick was Liam Scuab's cousin when he reneged your daughter. Quick was he after his days and nights of pleasure. Quick was my sister's death. Quick is death, mother! *[Losing control]* Quick, quick, quick is everything. Quick is marriage and quick is love

and quick is youth. Quick is Sive's womanhood before we know it. We can't ask all things nice, mother. The nicest of things happen quick, likewise the worst things. Quick is the best thought and thing of a man and gone before he knows it. Sive is lucky. She marries young with nothing to bear. She is only a girl and lucky, not a woman who will have been thinking of men.

Nanna: How is it all men will find words to save themselves? *[Sadly]* Women must pay for all happiness. That is their sorry shape, God help us.

Mike: *[Embarrassed]* Go aisy, mother!

Nanna: How can I go aisy when my own grandchild is for sale like an animal.

Mike: *[Shouts]* Am I to have no rest from ye? Are ye to be pricking and prodding always?

                 [MIKE opens the towel and places the soap, razor and brush in it. He folds the towel about them. He opens the front door to the yard. He takes the basin in one hand and the towel in the other, all in a passionate temper]

Mike: I will shave in the stable. There will be no nagging there!

                 [Exit MIKE. Slowly NANNA rises and closes the door after him. She goes to her own room]

Scene 2

[A fortnight later: night.

NANNA is alone. She fills a cup with milk from the tankard and sits close by the fire supping it. She lifts her head when she hears a delicate tapping at the door. The tapping is repeated when she does not answer immediately.

Slowly NANNA rises and goes to the door. She opens it.

Enter PATS]

Pats: I'm for the past hour at the four sides of the house watching and waiting to know would I see were you alone or was there someone here with you.

Nanna: I'm alone now, but I won't be for long. Mike will be from the bog shortly. He should be here now, whatever is keeping him.

Pats: 'Tis a good thing you are alone, anyway. *[Looks around]*
               And that there's no one to hear or see.

Nanna: There's a great air of trickery about you.

Pats: I saw the young girl, Sive, and the other one going the
               road to town airly in the day.

Nanna: Gone to buy the wedding clothes they are. £50 Dóta gave
               to buy the clothes and the drink for the wedding.

Pats: 'Tis about the wedding I came. Last night we made a plan
               in the caravan.

Nanna: What good is a plan now with the wedding tomorrow
               morning? The poor child is nearly out of her mind these
               past weeks.

Pats: At the caravan last night we were boiling a hare, the two
               of us, when who should arrive but Liam Scuab, that has a
               notion of Sive. A fine grámhar boy he is and his heart
               broke for love of the girl. He haven't laid eyes on her this
               long time.

Nanna: They keep her in the house all the time. There's always a
               one to watch her for fear she'd go out.

Pats: We thought of a plan, the three of us. And the plan is for
               the girl to steal out of the house tonight. He will be
               waiting for her at his own place.

Nanna: They watch her every minute.

Pats: After she go to bed, who will watch her?

Nanna: *[Excitedly]* 'Tis true, and there's a window to the room.

Pats: She will go in whatever clothes she will be wearing.
               Whisht . . . *[Pause]* Did you hear the sound of a step?

               [Both listen]

Nanna: 'Twas nothing! What else will she do?

Pats: She will go to the young man's house and they will be
               married as soon as possible.

Nanna: 'Twill be a great suck-in for all of them!

Pats:	Dóta, the farmer, has no business with a young girl. If he have a mind for women let him lie down with his own equals. He have no love for her. 'Tis the flesh of her he do be doting over. The young man have a true heart for her. She have a true heart for him. What more!
Nanna:	*[Giving him a coin]* God spare you to the roads you travel, Pats, for last night's work.
Pats:	'Twas done willing! God the Master makes His own reward!
Nanna:	Will they marry for sure in the morning?
Pats:	They will marry for sure. *[Takes a letter from his pocket]* When Sive comes from the town, give her this. There is writing inside that will tell her all. Let no one see you or they will rise to the scent. 'Tis the one chance we have.
Nanna:	*[Takes letter]* No one will see, I promise you. May God reward you for your goodness.
Pats:	'Tis a small thing to do for my sins and I have them in a plenty.
Nanna:	It might be the best if you went away now.
Pats:	There's more to go yet. When the women come from the town I will come again. Carthalawn, my son, will come too. We will sing a song, mar dhea, and give our blessing to the wedding. They will think that all is well if we pretend to expect the marriage of Dóta and the girl.
Nanna:	Go now and God speed you!
	[Suddenly MIKE appears in the doorway]
Mike:	I saw you coming, Pats Bocock, and I was watching you around the house. Like a spy you were; peeping and ducking like a spy!
	[NANNA hurriedly conceals letter, noticed by MIKE]
Pats:	I have gone through many a place in my travels but 'tis the first time I was called a spy.
Mike:	*[Entering]* What were you doing, then, around the house? Looking here and there and walking on your toes!

Pats: Thinking to steal a few eggs I was, but I changed my mind and said to myself that I would ask first before I went stealing.

Mike: No one would refuse you for an egg in this house.

Pats: Ah, sure, I know that well, but there is no fun in eating eggs unless they are stolen!

Mike: *[Suspicious]* You're making up, I'm thinkin'! I don't know what thing brought you but I'd say 'twas nothing good.

Pats: I've done you no harm but if I'm not wanted, I'll go.

Mike: And I've done you no harm and you were always welcome here and you always will. But come straight to the house from the road and there will be a warmer welcome for you. No man likes to have his house watched.

Pats: God forbid I should make a watch on a man or his house. A man who will spy upon another man or upon another man's woman is a troubled man. Goodnight to the two of ye and God bless.

Mike: And God bless to you!

         [Exits PATS]

Mike: What did he want, mother? What was the tinker doing here?

Nanna: Must a mother answer to her only son? Is there no respect for old people?

Mike: I have always tried to please you. I never gave lip. It is hard to be a good son and a good husband under the same roof. *[Sits down and leans forward, looking into space]*

Nanna: We were happy and content here before that woman came into the house. Where is the love you used to have for Sive? Everywhere you went you used to take her with you. You were better than a father to her. Where is the promise you gave to your sister?

Mike: *[Harried]* Will you not be tormenting me again. Didn't I say to you that a horse can't be guided two roads at once. *[Suspiciously]* And what is it you were hiding from me when I came in? You expect me to be open with you while you play trickery with the tinker. Tell me what it was you were hiding?

Nanna: I have nothing to hide from you.

Mike: There you are now, telling me lies again!

Nanna: I'll tell you the truth if you'll promise on your word as my son that 'twill be secret.

Mike: I promise on my word as your son! *[Solemnly]*

Nanna: *[Withdrawing letter]* 'Tis a letter from Liam Scuab to Sive. There is no harm in it. Only saying goodbye to her in his own way. 'Tis the kind of notion young people have! Little faldals between them.

Mike: Why was Pats Bocock prowling in the yard?

Nanna: He was afraid to give the letter to anyone but me. Sure, if your wife or Thomasheen Seán Rua got hold of it, wouldn't they only set fire to it.

Mike: Are you sure there's nothing more in it?

Nanna: Wouldn't I tell you if there was?

Mike: *[Reflectively]* Mmmmmh!

Nanna: And would I be such a fool as to show it to you if there was anything more in it?

Mike: That's true, I suppose.

Nanna: Mike, my son, I know that in your own heart you're against this match. I know you do be thinking your own thoughts about it, about that little wraneen of a man and your sister's child that you love.

Mike: Mother, will you leave me alone! Ye'll set me out of my mind between all of ye.

Nanna: Give her this letter yourself, Mike.

Mike: Oh, no!

Nanna: She will never get it so because they will be watching for me to leave my room and they would see me giving it to her.

Mike: I . . . I . . . can't, mother! *[Dread sincerity]*

Nanna: 'Twill be the last bit of comfort or consolation she'll have from this night to her grave.

Mike: Good God! Why are ye all at me!

Nanna: If you have a bit of love left in you for Sive and me, you will take this letter and give it to her. What harm will it do? Sure, there's nothing inside in it only a last goodbye and wishing her joy for her wedding.

Mike: Mother, I would do anything in my power, but . . .

Nanna: Then do this small thing I ask you. No one will know and you will bring joy to your mother's heart and maybe a small bit of joy for Sive.

Mike: Give me the letter!

Nanna: *[Handing letter to him]* God bless you, my son.

Mike: *[Crosses to the fireplace for his glasses]* I'm doing wrong by Mena, but it can't do any harm if he's only saying goodbye.

Nanna: And you won't read it?

Mike: *[Suddenly]* Why . . . why shouldn't I read it?

Nanna: Ah, wouldn't you know yourself the little private things they had between them. If the letter was opened she would only throw it in your face and she'd hate you more for it. Leave the letter sealed. It is a kind of a thing a girl would like to have for keepsake after she'd be married.

Mike: *[In a quandary]* You're very anxious I shouldn't read it.

Nanna: Did I read it myself? And I had it before you. You made a promise you'd give it. Stick to your promise.

Mike: *[Irritably]* I'll stick to my promise.

Nanna: God will reward you, Mike . . . *[The dogs bark]* You're a good son in your heart.

[NANNA exits quickly to her room.

MIKE looks at the letter for a few moments. He places it on the mantlepiece and looks at it for a moment longer. He takes a brush and crosses to sweep around the meal sacks.

The door opens and THOMASHEEN enters, dressed as usual. He gives his usual furtive glances]

Thomasheen: There was a great housekeeper lost in you. You have the gameze and the antics of a woman the way you handle the brush.

Mike: You are in great fettle at the heel of the day!

Thomasheen: What is the news by you?

Mike: News! What news would I have, man, that was in the depth of the bog all day, footin' turf?

Thomasheen: Are they back from town yet?

Mike: *[Innocently]* And what would anyone be doing in town?

Thomasheen: *[Laughs]* Oh, wisha Mike, will you not be playing Moll the Wag? Who is in town but herself and the girl. Didn't I see Seán Dóta giving Mena £50 to buy finery for tomorrow's wedding.

Mike: God gave you great eyes.

Thomasheen: He gave them to the right man. £50 was a great bundle of money for a bit of clothes.

Mike: *[Defensively]* It was given for Sive's clothes and it will be spent on Sive's clothes.

Thomasheen: *[Crossing to the fire]* Given for Sive but the two of us know that Mena will have £40 out of the £50 for herself.

Mike: You're a great mind for putting and taking with sums of money.

Thomasheen: God gave me that, too. Sure, what harm is it if herself makes a few pounds in the buying of the clothes. Doesn't she deserve it. She worked hard for the wedding, God knows. *[Turns and walks towards window]*

> *[MIKE does not answer. He crosses to the fire. He glances around to see THOMASHEEN looking out of the window and furtively takes the letter to hide in his pocket. As he is doing so, THOMASHEEN turns suddenly]*

Thomasheen: What is that?

Mike: Nothing!

Thomasheen: Since when did Mike Glavin start putting nothing into his pocket?

Mike: Well, if your mind is that curious, it was a letter, although it's none of your business or mine but as little.

Thomasheen: *[Laughs]* Until I have a hundred sovereigns in my breast pocket, I will make business out of everything. Who is the letter for?

Mike: Sive.

Thomasheen: Sive, is it? And who is it from?

Mike: How would I know? Bocock the tinker handed it in, passing the way. I'm keeping it for her.

Thomasheen: *[Alert and serious. Then, with alarm]* And the letter is for Sive?

Mike: That's what I told you! Somebody wishing her well, I suppose, on the eve of her wedding.

Thomasheen: And what will you do with the letter?

Mike: I will give it to Sive, of course, when she lands from town. What else would I do with it?

Thomasheen: It comes to me now and again about you!

Mike: What comes to you?

Thomasheen: It comes to me that you are the greatest lump of a fool, of an eejit, of a dull amu, in the seven parishes. You shouldn't be trusted with a quenched match. How do you know what is in the letter? Wishing her well, how are you? If you ever get out of the bog and put a few days aside for journeying there is an asylum for lunatics where you could put down a bit of time without doing youself any harm.

Mike: *[Frowns in misunderstanding]* It is only a letter.

Thomasheen: *[Mimics MIKE]* Only a letter!

Mike: What harm could be in a few words of writing?

Thomasheen: *[Patiently]* Aaah! My dotey God! What should be in it but thoughts to disturb her young head the night before her marriage. Have you no knowledge of the way a woman do be the night before? Turning and twisting and wondering if she is doing right or wrong. A woman never knows from one minute to the next what way her mind is going to act. 'Tis their affliction. 'Tis the way they are made. You must make up the mind for them. You must whip them up and keep them going, or, like a giddy heifer on the road to the fair, the next thing you know she'll let a screech out of her, cock her tail up high in the air and break through the first gap in a hedge into some other man's land, and be content there.

Mike: What signifies that?

Thomasheen: Little you know! Open the letter and read out the contents of it.

Mike: It isn't your letter.

Thomasheen: Will you take it out of your pocket and not be playing the gom?

Mike: *[Taking out the letter]* But it is Sive's letter and it is marked 'Private' with a red pencil.

Thomasheen: If it was marked with green, white and yellow and sealed with a bishop's ring it will have to be opened. Will you not be tormenting me now, and open it.

Mike: *[Yielding]* But, sure, what harm . . . ?

Thomasheen: *[Assumes a tearful tone, in mockery]* Will you open it or you'll drive me to Gleann na nGealt where your own equals do be.

Mike: *[Pause]* Isn't she getting married tomorrow. Let her have the letter. 'Tis private, look . . .

[He holds the letter at arm's length. With a swift adroit movement THOMASHEEN snatches the letter and tears it open. He takes the sheets of folded notepaper from the envelope and opens them. He looks at them and hands them to MIKE]

Thomasheen: Read!

Mike: Read yourself!

Thomasheen: I had no time for schoolin' when I was a boy. Read it now an' don't be makin' trouble for yourself.

[MIKE takes the letter hesitantly and peruses the first page]

Mike: *[Disgustedly]* You read it! That's Sive's letter.

[MIKE hands the letter back to THOMASHEEN who holds up his hand in rejection]

Thomasheen: *[Embarrassed]* Will you not be mocking. The letter is only like the print of a bird's claw in snow to me. *[Then, firmly]* You read it out or I'll take it the road down to Seamus Dónal's.

Mike: *[Resignedly]* All right! All right! I'll read it but it goes against the grain by me.

[MIKE takes a pair of spectacles from his breast-pocket and commences to read. His voice is slow, laborious, hardly doing justice to the letter]

Mike: *[Reading]* 'My dearest Sive . . .'

Thomasheen: Aaah!

Mike: *[Concentrates on letter which presents him with a difficult problem. Reading]* 'My dearest Sive, you may remember the last time I spoke to you when I met you coming from school . . .'

Thomasheen: Go on! *[He enjoys himself beyond measure]* Go on, let you! Do it say there who 'tis from?

Mike: *[Finds end of letter and reads]* 'Yours eternally, Liam.'

Thomasheen: Oh, boys! Oh, boys!

Mike: *[Coughs, reads]* '. . . I have heard from Carthalawn and Pats Bocock, the tinker-poets, that you are getting married to Seán Dóta, the farmer . . .'

Thomasheen: Would you say now that it was a private letter? *[Triumphantly]* Would you say now that it shouldn't be read? *[Contemptuously]* Go on, man, and read the contents of it.

Mike: . . . 'Sive, my dearest Sive, I find it impossible to believe that you are marrying this wizened little man of your own accord . . . *[reading faster]* . . . do you not remember the nights, the starry nights, we spent together in the deep of the bog. There was the quiet and the peace of what we felt for each other. I loved you then, Sive. I love you now . . .'

Thomasheen: He did, indeed! Aha! the scoundrel! Breaking up honest homes. Has he no love for the law of the land and the voice of the priest?

Mike: Will you hold your tongue and let me finish! *[Worried tone]* 'You are certain to think here that I am beginning to wax poetic . . .'

Thomasheen: Wax? *[Loudly]* He's wax from head to heel! *[Knowingly]* He will never have a woman the way he is going about it! There is no wax in the ketching of women. There is the ketchin' of a hoult until she is winded. That's the time for words with a woman.

Mike: Do you want me to read the letter or will I leave it?

Thomasheen: Go on! Go on, blast you! You're mad for the word on paper. *[MIKE turns over a page and continues, for a moment master of the situation because he can read, also obviously impressed by the sincerity of the letter]*

Mike: *[Reading]* '. . . so I have made a decision with regard to you. I believe you are being forced into this marriage against your will. If that is the case and I hope with all my heart that it is, I beg of you Sive, to do as I say. Tonight when they have all gone to bed, steal away quietly and come to my house. I will be waiting there for you. We will drive straight to the city and be married there the first thing. Remember, I will wait for you through the whole night . . .'

Thomasheen: Oh, the juice of the roses! Oh, the blood of the grape!

Mike: *[Reading]* '. . . if you do not come, I will take it that you are content with your choice.'

Thomasheen: Oh, the moon and the stars!

Mike: 'If this be so, goodbye and God keep you safe. Yours eternally, Liam.'

Thomasheen: Ah! They had it well planned! God always finds out a rogue. Trying to steal away the poor innocent girl in the dark of the night!

[MIKE folds the letter and places it on the table. He takes off his glasses, and lifts the torn envelope from the ground. It is obvious that the letter has rattled him]

Mike: What will we do?

Thomasheen: I don't know! *[As MIKE is pre-occupied with his thoughts, THOMASHEEN takes the letter in the tongs and burns it over the fire]*

Mike: *[Angrily]* What are you doing?

[MIKE tries to snatch the letter but THOMASHEEN roughly pushes him away. He drops the letter and envelope to the ground]

Thomasheen: Leave it burn! Leave it burn! What she don't know won't trouble her. Our man will have a long wait below. *[He crushes the burning letter under his foot]*

Mike: The letter was Sive's!

Thomasheen: Will you hold your tongue, you bloody óinseach! Keep your gob shut. There's the noise of the pony and car on the bóithrín. Forget about the letter. You don't know the harm you might cause. When she comes, pretend nothing.

Mike: God direct me, but am I doing right by the girl at all? *[He says this half to himself]*

Thomasheen: In the honour of God will you be one way or the other, will you? . . . Will you? . . . *[Raises his voice]* You're like an oul' hen, dodgin' an' dartin', not knowin' what way to turn. Straighten yourself out, man, and be your age for one time in your life.

[THOMASHEEN goes to the window and looks out]

Thomasheen: They're in the yard . . . they've the car loaded with stuff . . . Aha! Cases of porter! The devil knows what!

SIVE

[THOMASHEEN turns to the door and rubs his hands together with great delight. MENA enters the kitchen. She carries a large, brown-papered parcel under one arm and a smaller parcel under the other]

Mena: *[Crossly]* 'Tis a wonder one of ye didn't open the door when ye saw me coming with my hands full.

Mike: Where is Sive?

Mena: She is coming.

[SIVE enters and stands self-consciously in her new clothes]

Mike: There's style.

Mena: Go out to the car and bring in the boxes and don't be standing there with your hands hanging.

[Without a word, both men go out, MIKE in the lead. SIVE takes off a pair of new high-heeled shoes which she is wearing and rubs her soles fondly, religiously, with her right hand, balancing with her left hand resting on the table. Slowly she takes off coat and hat. She wears a smart blue frock underneath. She takes coat and hat to the room near the hearth. MENA, the parcels in her hands, goes after SIVE into the room.

Immediately MIKE and THOMASHEEN enter, carrying a crate of stout between them. MIKE removes a chair from between the dresser and the door and puts the box in its place. He goes to dresser, finds a bottle-opener and deftly uncaps two bottles, one of which he hands to THOMASHEEN. He puts the opener in his pocket]

Mike: Go mbeirimid beó!

Thomasheen: Good luck to us all and bad luck to no one!

[Both drink heartily from the bottles, lower them, lift them secondly in unison and drain the bottles, which they return to the box. They then hurry out to the yard again.

SIVE enters the kitchen wearing a pair of low shoes. She sits on a chair near the fire holding her hands in her lap awkwardly.]

THOMASHEEN and MIKE return with a second crate which they put on top of the first. Both look cautiously at SIVE and then at each other. SIVE does not look up at them. MENA arrives into the kitchen]

Mena: Will ye hurry up, for God's sake, and bring in the other boxes.

[Both men go out again and MENA places a hand on SIVE'S shoulder]

Mena: We will have a bit to eat now. There are sausages and rashers and sweet cake to follow.

Sive: *[Without looking up]* I'm not hungry. *[Tired and dispirited]* I think I'll go to bed instead. My head is on fire.

Mena: You haven't put a bite inside of you all day. How do you think you will feel if you don't eat?

Sive: I don't feel any desire for food. *[Absently]* I would like to lie down.

[MIKE and THOMASHEEN enter the kitchen again carrying a large tea-chest between them]

Mena: Put it down there! *[They place it aside]*

Mike: I think I will chance a bottle of stout after that.

Thomasheen: It never did harm!

[MENA looks with disapproval at him when MIKE extracts two bottles from the upper crate. He returns and hands one to THOMASHEEN, having opened both]

Mena: *[To MIKE, with caution]* Don't you know what that stuff does to you? We'll be having you puking and choking for the rest of the night like a sick cat.

[THOMASHEEN and MIKE drink from the bottles]

Mike: 'Tis all right, woman! 'Tis all right!

Thomasheen: Is the stomach delicate with you?

Mike: *[To SIVE, in a kind tone]* Will you have a drop of lemonade, Sive, or maybe a suppeen of wine to warm you?

Sive: *[Sighs]* No! I have no mind for it.

Mena: *[Not crossly]* And what will you have? You're not hungry and you're not thirsty. Is there anything you have a mind for?

Sive: *[Shakes her head]* No, nothing!

Mena: I don't know what to say to you.

Sive: *[Rises, slowly, wearily]* I think I'll go to bed now.

Mena: The bed is made and ready for you. Maybe you will feel like something later on.

[SIVE walks slowly to her room. MENA watches her hard-eyed. Exit SIVE. MENA goes to dresser and puts three saucers on table]

Mena: Will you go out and untackle the pony. Do you want the poor animal to die on his feet?

[MIKE finishes his bottle, places it in crate and hurries out closing the door. MENA returns to dresser and puts out three cups on the saucers]

Thomasheen: Well?

Mena: Well, what?

Thomasheen: Is everything going right with the girl?

Mena: I told you there is no need to worry about that part of it. Mind you collect what is due to us in the morning.

Thomasheen: When the ring is on her finger, I'll handle the money. There is no fear Seán Dóta will part with a farthing before his time.

Mena: Ah, you needn't tell me!

Thomasheen: He gave you £50 to buy finery. *[He advances with bottle in hand]*

Mena: It was wanted!

Thomasheen: You could buy a shop for £50.

Mena: He gave me the money, me to do what I liked with it. I bought the best, and if there is a shilling or two left over who is better entitled to it than me?

Thomasheen: There was a letter from Liam Scuab for Sive!

Mena: What?

Thomasheen: He was for giving it to her. *[He indicates outside where* MIKE *has gone]*

Mena: The fool! Where is the letter now? Where is it?

Thomasheen: Calm yourself, woman! Calm yourself! I took it from him and burned it.

Mena: A good night's work!

Thomasheen: And what way is the old woman?

Mena: I am from the house all day. She never appeared yesterday or the day before.

Thomasheen: Just as well.

> *[The door opens and* MIKE *enters. Immediately he takes a bottle from the crate.* THOMASHEEN *drains his quickly and puts it in the crate. He takes the bottle from* MIKE'S *hand and hands another from crate to* MIKE.
>
>   *Leisurely* MIKE *thrusts his hand into his trousers pocket and produces the opener.* THOMASHEEN *holds the bottle steady whilst* MIKE *uncaps it.* MIKE *uncaps his own and sits on the sacks.*
>
>   THOMASHEEN *sits upon the tea chest. Both raise the bottles to their mouths and quaff deeply]*

Mena: Ye will have nothing left the way ye're going. Tomorrow is to come yet, take care.

Mike: *[Lifting his bottle to remonstrate]* Only a few oul' bottles of porter.

Thomasheen: *[Who is a joy unto himself]* We will be in the middle of plenty soon!

Mike: There is company, the road up. I saw him far down. . . .

Mena: *[Much interested]* Who is that?

Mike: Dóta! *[Lifts bottle and drinks]*

Thomasheen: Long life!

Mike: Long life to us!

Mena: Seán Dóta?

Mike: Seán Dóta, the farmer! *[Drinks]*

Mena: Will you go aisy with that! D'you remember the last time you drank porter. D'you remember the state of the room after you. You're like a pet banbh snugglin' and sucklin' for all the good it's doing you. Will you ever come to the age of sense?

Thomasheen: *[Solemnly]* It might be safer to give no drink to what's comin'! If he had a fall on the road and gave over life wouldn't we be in a nice state with the whole country laughing at us in the morning.

Mena: He's in safe-keeping here. *[Raises her head and listens]* Hold aisy! He's down on the door!

[THOMASHEEN suddenly comes to his feet and withdraws to the far side of the working table. Delicately he lifts bottle to his lips and drinks slowly, keeping his eye on the door. There is a timid knock on the door. MENA goes to it and opens door. SEÁN DÓTA enters, apologetically and with his customary half-laugh he salutes them]

Thomasheen: Mind your step, Seán.

Mena: Seán, will you sit up to the fire?

Seán Dóta: *[Who is dressed as before, raises a deprecatory hand and laughs apologetically]* No fire for me, thank you. No fire. *[He surveys kitchen, hands behind back]*

Thomasheen: *[Closing the front door]* Soon enough you will have the fire to your side, you diggle, you!

Seán Dóta: *[Laughs apologetically]* Ho-ho! the joker! *[He shakes his head]*

Mena: Will you sit down? You must be a bundle of nerves in wait for morning?

Seán Dóta: *[Laughingly]* Oh, wisha, indeed now! I came to see if all was right.

Mike: Rest yourself Seán! All is right!

                [SEAN sits on the chair to the right of the kitchen table]

Mena: Sive is resting in her room

Seán Dóta: The bit of rest is good.

Mike: The weather is holding up fine.

Seán Dóta: The rain is threatening this long time. *[Laughs]* When 'twill
                fall 'twill fall heavy, I'm thinking.'Twill be no harm. Won't
                it give rise to growth.

Thomasheen: True for you.

                *[MENA goes to dresser and takes out small plates which she
                distributes about table. She bends to the lower part and
                takes out a large plate of home-baked bread. The men
                keep talking]*

Mike: There is talk of the milk rising.

Seán Dóta: *[Laughs]* No harm indeed to rise it. Great waste going into
                the feeding of cows. Ye are celebrating, I see.

Mike: So well we might, it being the night it is!

Seán Dóta: *[Laughs]* Oho!

                *[MENA takes knives and spoons from dresser and puts them
                on table. She slices the bread]*

Mike: Will you take something yourself, Seán?

Seán Dóta: *[Laughs]* Oho! *[He casts a quick glance at the crate of
                bottles]*

Mike: It never poisoned a man yet.

Seán Dóta: *[Laughs]* Well . . . I suppose . . .

Mena: *[Turns to SEÁN, with knife upraised in her hand]* No man
                should taste the taste of drink the night before his marriage.

Mike: That's true.

Mena: I will pour out a nice bottle of lemonade for you now
                Seán.

Seán Dóta: Don't mind me! I'll sit here for myself.

Mena: I'll put a place at the table for you.

[MENA goes to dresser and puts out another cup and saucer on the table. She then takes a jug from the dresser and fills it from the tank, drying the bottom of it with a cloth. She puts the jug on the table]

Mena: *[Raises a hand for silence]* Whisht yeerselves!

[They all listen attentively, then unmistakably comes the sound of a bodhrán in the distance, growing in volumn. THOMASHEEN slips unobtrusively to the fire and puts his back to it, fearfully]

Thomasheen: 'Tis Bocock and his son.

Mike: Come in, let you.

[The tapping of the stick is heard upon the door, in time with the bodhrán. PATS and CARTHALAWN appear in the doorway. CARTHALAWN is playing and singing]

Carthalawn: Come now listen while I sing
To the blessing that I bring
To the bridegroom and his lovely bride so fair
May they dwell in wedded joy
May they ever hear the cry
Of a new big bouncing baby every year.

Mike: Great work! Great work! Ye're welcome to these parts. Will ye drink porter?

[MENA stands by, arms folded, scowling]

Pats: We will, indeed! We saw the boxes coming up the tar-road with the porter-bottles buck-jumping inside in them. I would follow a box of porter to the gates of hell and beyond if I was dry.

[MIKE takes two bottles from the crate, opens them, and hands them to CARTHALAWN and PATS. He replaces his own empty bottle and opens another for himself]

Pats: That we might never want!

*[PATS toasts MIKE, MIKE quaffs his bottle. PATS and
CARTHALAWN empty their bottles at one swallow. MIKE
returns to his chair with his bottle]*

Mike: Let ye sit down.

Pats: We would sooner stand.

Mike: Ye know all here?

Pats: We do, indeed.

Mike: Ye know Seán Dóta, who is for marriage in the morning?

Pats: *[Meaningly]* We know the farmer.

Mike: What is the news from the country?

Pats: There is money making everywhere. The face of the country
                 is changing.The small man with the one cow and the pig
                 and the bit of bog is coming into his own. He is pulling
                 himself up out of the mud and the dirt of the years. He is
                 coming away from the dunghill and the smoky corner.
                 The shopkeeper is losing his stiffness. 'Tis only what I see
                 in my travels. The farmer will be the new lord of the land.
                 What way will he rule? What way will he hould up under
                 the new riches? There will be great changes everywhere.
                 The servant boy is wearing the collar and the tie. The
                 servant girl is painting and powdering and putting silkified
                 stockings on her feet and wearing frilly small clothes under
                 her dress. 'Tis only what I see in my travels. The servant
                 will kick off the traces and take to the high road. Money
                 will be in a-plenty. *[He points at SEÁN DÓTA]* The likes of
                 him will be the new lords of the land. God help the land!

Mena: You're full of dare to insult a dacent respectable man in
                 my house.

Pats: 'Tis only what I see in my travels, a-woman — only what I
                 see in my travels.

Thomasheen: Well, ye can be travelling out of here now. The cheek of
                 ye!

Pats: Carthalawn! Your best! *[He taps with his stick]* Your mighty
                 best!

[PATS taps with his stick again and CARTHALAWN takes up the time. Then the sounds decrease and CARTHALAWN sings]

Carthalawn: *[Singing]* May he screech with awful thirst
May his brains and eyeballs burst
That melted amadán, that big bostoon,
May the fleas consume his bed
And the mange eat up his head,
That blackman from the mountain, Seánín
Rua.

Mike: Great work! Great work! *[He slaps his knee with his hand in glee]*

Seán Dóta: Ho-ho! Ho-ho!

[THOMASHEEN fumes with rage. MENA scowls at the tinkers]

Mike: Ye never lost it! 'Pon my word, ye never lost it!

[SEÁN DÓTA rises]

Seán Dóta: I will be for the road. God knows, I will have an early start in the morning.

Mena: Will you wait till I call Sive up from the room. She will be dying to see you before you go .

Seán Dóta: *[Changes his mind quickly and sits on the chair again]* By God! I'll wait a minute or two, so!

[MENA goes into the room by the hearth. PATS sweeps off his hat and holds it in front of SEÁN]

Pats: Something to bring luck to you! A handful of silver!

Seán Dóta: How soft you have it! Money for nothing, how are you?

[PATS retreats dignified to stand in line with his son]

Mike: You must be getting tired, Seán? I know what is the feeling of a day before marriage.

Pats: It will be a rest for the poor man to marry.

Seán Dóta: *[Laughs]* A rest?

Pats: The young girl will be the death of you.

Seán Dóta: How dare you! How dare you, tinker?

Pats: A squeeze out of a lively young girl would stop your heart, old man. Carthalawn, your best! Your mighty best!

Carthalawn: *[Sings]*   May his hens lay clods and stones
May the east wind blight his bones
May warts and welts waylay him by the score.
Now I swear upon this verse
He'll be travelling soon by hearse
And we'll never see Seán Dóta anymore.

Mena: *[Re-entering hysterically]* She's gone! There's a bundle of clothes under the quilt where she should be lying. She's after stealing away on us!

Thomasheen: *[Seizes her by the arm, roughly]* What are you screeching about? Catch a hould of yourself.

Mena: She's gone, I tell you! The window of the room is open!

Thomasheen: Did she take baggage with her?

Mena: No! . . . No! . . . Nothing! not even a shoe for her feet.

Thomasheen: Would she have stolen around to the old woman's room?

[MENA breaks from his grasp and hurries to NANNA's room to look in]

Thomasheen: *[Loudly]* Well? Is she there?

Mike: *[Stands up]* Where could she have gone at this hour of the night, without a shoe or a coat on her?

Pats: There was something a while ago and we coming up from the cross.

Thomasheen: Out with it! What?

Pats: *[Frowning]* It may be that my eyes would be fooling me but I thought I saw the figure of a girl flashing across the bog near the end of the cutaway where the deep holes do be. I thought it might be a shadow.

Mena: *[Composed again]* And why didn't you say so when you came?

Pats:	How was I to know if the sight of my eyes was going or coming? It was only now that you talk about the girl that I think it might have been the girl, Sive.
Thomasheen:	You oul bocock! You oul' dirty twisted bocock! Damn well you knew!
Pats:	I did not know, and what is it to me if all the people of the parish ran over the bog in the middle of the night with bare feet.
Mena:	What if she fell into a hole . . . Oh, my God! *[She shrieks at MIKE]* Find her! Find her! . . . Hurry yourself!
Mike:	I'll get a lantern in the stable . . .

[MENA rushes to the room by the fireplace and returns almost immediately with the rubber waders. MIKE kicks off his shoes and pulls on the waders]

Thomasheen:	I will go with you.
Seán Dóta:	I will go along with ye.
Mena:	Stay, Seán! I will not stay here alone by myself. Stay, somebody. Stay with me. I won't be alone.

[From outside, a frantic voice is heard]

Liam Scuab:	Show light! . . . Show light! . . . Leave open the door . . . I am coming over the bog.

[THOMASHEEN opens the door fully. MENA hurries with the oil lamp to the door. MIKE hurries to the door. All exchange frightened glances.

They retreat from the door as LIAM draws near. Their faces are horrified as they stand back.

Enter LIAM. He is bareheaded and his clothes are wet. His face is ghastly pale. In his arms he carries SIVE. Her hair is plastered to her head and her slight body hangs limp in LIAM's arms. LIAM advances without looking left or right. At the table he stops.

PATS comes forward and with his stick sweeps the table clean. The ware clatters on the ground breaking the silence. Reverently LIAM lays the motionless body on the table.

The water drips on the floor from both LIAM and SIVE. LIAM folds SIVE's hand across her breast. MENA replaces the lamp]

Liam: A cloth to dry her hair!

[MENA hands LIAM a cloth. THOMASHEEN edges in to look at the body, then horrified, edges slyly away and exits, looking around him furtively. He is noticed only by SEÁN DÓTA who follows him, backing, sneaking, to the door, SEÁN exits]

Liam: *[Tearfully]* I saw her running across the bog with only the little frock against the cold of the night. She ran like the wind and she letting cries out of her that would rend your heart. *[Filled with sorrow]* I called after her but she would not stop. She took her own life. It was a while before I found her. The poor tormented child.

Mena: Drowned, dead.

[LIAM turns suddenly on MENA, blazing with anger]

Liam: *[Cries in anguish]* You killed her! You . . .You . . .you . . . you killed her! You horrible filthy bitch! That the hand of Jesus may strike you dead where you stand. You heartless wretch that hunted the poor little girl to her grave.

[MENA retreats, shocked, before him, her hand stupidly covering her mouth]

Liam: *[Shrieks]* Go away! . . . Go away! . . . You are polluting the pure spirit of the child with your nearness. Go away, witch!

[LIAM raises the towel clenched in his fist to strike MENA. MENA hurries away back to her room, LIAM begins to dry SIVE'S hair with the cloth, lovingly and with care]

Liam: The beautiful hair of her! *[He takes her hand]* The lovely silky white of her!

Mike: *[Stupidly, idiotically]* The priest . . . we must go for the priest . . . she must have the priest . . . . Holy ground . . . she must be buried in holy ground . . . the priest . . . . I must go for the priest . . .

[LIAM gives MIKE a scalding look]

Liam: Go for the priest then! . . . Go on! . . . Go!

[MIKE seizes LIAM by the two hands]

Mike: I can't go alone! . . . There's no luck in going for a priest alone. You know the old saying . . .

[MIKE is foolish, babbling now. LIAM shakes off MIKE's hands violently. He seizes MIKE by the hand and drags him to the door]

Liam: Come on! . . . I'll lead you past where she was drowned. You'll be on the tar road then. You'll find company.

[They both go out leaving PATS and CARTHALAWN alone with SIVE. After a moment CARTHALAWN goes forward and touches SIVE's face with his hand. His face is sad as he looks at her. After a few seconds PATS taps with his stick and CARTHALAWN draws away slowly. Both men stand to attention. Then, gently, the stick taps, the knuckles very gently tap the bodhrán to slow time. Slow of voice and tenderly CARTHALAWN sings. PATS looks at him tenderly]

Carthalawn: *[Singing]*   Oh, come all good men and true,
A sad tale I'll tell to you
All of a maiden fair, who died this day;
Oh, they drowned lovely Sive,
She would not be a bride
And they laid her for to bury in the clay

[They turn slowly and march slowly in step through the door, CARTHALAWN still singing gently]

Carthalawn: *[Singing]*   Oh, come all good men and true
A sad tale I'll tell to you
All of a maiden fair, who died this day.
Oh, they murdered lovely Sive,
She would not be a bride,
And they laid her dead, to bury in the clay.

[The singing fades, slowly, slowly, as the light fades in the kitchen.

    NANNA, in the faint light comes slowly from her room and goes to where SIVE is lying. She bows her head over the dead body and weeps silently.

    The singing fades away altogether]

[Final Curtain]

The Field

This edited two act version of *The Field* was first presented in the Abbey Theatre, Dublin on Monday 9 February 1987.

LEAMY FLANAGAN	Darragh Kelly
BIRD O'DONNELL	Dónall Farmer
MICK FLANAGAN	John Olohan
MRS BUTLER	Áine Ní Mhuirí
MAIMIE FLANAGAN	Catherine Byrne
BULL McCABE	Niall Tóibín
TADHG McCABE	Brendan Conroy
SERGEANT LEAHY	Niall O'Brien
WILLIAM DEE	Macdara Ó Fátharta
DANDY McCABE	Eamon Kelly
MRS McCABE	Maura O'Sullivan
FR MURPHY	Des Nealon
THE FLANAGAN CHILDREN	Aoife Conroy
	Neilí Conroy
	Ruaidhrí Conroy
	Tom Lawlor
	Kerry-Ellen Lawlor
VILLAGE GIRLS	Aisling Tóibín
	Siobhán Maguire
THE BISHOP'S VOICE	Des Cave

DIRECTOR   Ben Barnes
DESIGNER   Tim Reed
LIGHTING DESIGNER   Rupert Murray
MUSIC   Ronan Guilfoyle

The Field was first produced by Gemini Productions at the Olympia Theatre, Dublin on 1 November 1965.

ACT ONE
Scene 1

[Action takes place in the bar of a public-house in Carraigthomond, a small village in the south-west of Ireland.

LEAMY FLANAGAN is playing pitch and toss with his younger brothers and sisters. Enter the BIRD O'DONNELL]

Bird: Give us a half of whiskey for God's sake, Leamy, to know would anything put a bit of heat in me. Leamy, do you hear me talking to you?

Leamy: 'Tis freezing!

Bird: 'Tis weather for snowmen and Eskimos. Where's your father? This place is getting more like Las Vegas with all the gambling going on.

Leamy: He's gone down to O'Connor's for the paper . . . That'll be half-a-dollar.

Bird: Take your time, will you? Why aren't ye all at school?

Leamy: Still on our Easter holidays. How's trade?

Bird: Same as always . . . lousy!

[Enter MICK FLANAGAN scattering the children]

Mick: Go upstairs, your dinner is ready. *[To LEAMY]* I thought I told you to sweep out the shop!

Leamy: It's nearly finished.

Mick: You've been long enough about it. Right Nellie, up to Muddy. Good morning, Bird.

Bird: Good morning, Mick.

Mick: Did you clean out the store?

Leamy: I've done the half of it.

Mick: The half of it! — I told you to do the whole of it.

Leamy: I had to look after the kids while my mother was feeding the baby.

Mick: 'Tis too fond you are of hanging about with women and children. 'Tis a daughter you should have been not a son. *[Discovering another child]* And what are you doing hiding under the table, you little divil? *[To LEAMY]* Go and ask your mother will the dinner be ready soon.

Leamy: Yes, Da.

Mick: And finish off that store or you'll hear all about it from me.

Leamy: Yes, Da.

              [Exit LEAMY, BIRD whistles]

Mick: In the name of goodness, will you cut out that bloody whistling! One would swear you were a canary.

              [The Whistler, whose name is 'BIRD' O'DONNELL, looks at MICK in surprise]

Bird: *[Throwing rings at a ring-board]* I thought you liked whistling?

Mick: Whistling, yes. I like whistling. But that bloody noise you're making isn't whistling.

              [Laughter from girls. BIRD comes to the counter. He has thrown two rings and leaves the other four on the counter]

Mick: C'mon girls, upstairs.

Bird: Give me another half-one. It might improve my pipes.

Mick: Have you the price of it?

              [BIRD draws some change from his pocket and places it on the counter]

Mick: *[Counts money first, fills whiskey]* Who did you take down now?

Bird: Take down! That's illegal, that is! I could get you put in jail for that. A pity I hadn't a witness. 'Twould pay me better than calf-buying.

              [MICK places whiskey on counter and takes price of it which he deposits in cash register. BIRD scoops up the rest of the money]

Mick:	There must be great money in calf-buying.
Bird:	Not as much as there is in auctioneering.
Mick:	*[Goes to the stove, to poke and put fuel in it]* Very funny! Very funny! Don't forget I have to use my head all the time.
Bird:	*[Leftish along counter]* Not half as much as I do. Did you ever try to take down a small farmer?
	[BIRD sits in angle of bar watching what is going on. Enter a small dumpy woman wearing a black-coloured coat. She is piled with parcels. She is MAGGIE BUTLER, a widow]
Bird:	Good morning, ma'am.
Mick:	Good morning, ma'am. Ah! Is it Mrs Butler? I didn't see you with a dog's age.
Maggie:	Good morning to you, Mr Flanagan. I'm afraid I don't be in the village very often.
Mick:	What will I get for you?
Maggie:	*[Laughs at the idea]* 'Tisn't drink I'm looking for, Mr Flanagan. 'Tis other business entirely that brought me. I've been thinking of payin' you a call for some time.
Mick:	You wouldn't be selling property now, by any chance? The bit of land or the house or maybe both?
Maggie:	No, not the house! Lord save us, do you want me on the side of the road or stuck in a room in some back lane in Carraigthomond? 'Tis the field I came to see you about. I'm a poor widow woman and I want the best price I can get. They say you're an honest man to get the last half-penny for a person.
Mick:	*[Suddenly expansive, comes from behind the counter]* Sit down here, Maggie girl. I can guarantee you, you won't be wronged in this house. You came to the right spot. Am I right, Bird?
Bird:	No better man. As straight as a telephone pole.
Mick:	I suppose you know the Bird O'Donnell?
Maggie:	Only to see. How do you do, sir.

Mick: How would you like a little drop of something before we get down to business? Something to put a stir in the heart.

Maggie: Oh, Lord save us, no! I never touches it! Since the day my poor husband died, I never put a drop of drink to my lips. We used often take a bottle of stout together. *[Sadly]* But that was once upon a time. The Lord have mercy on the dead.

Mick & Bird: The Lord have mercy on the dead!

Mick: 'Tis easy to see you're a moral woman. 'Twould be a brighter world if there were more like you.

Bird: That's true, God knows. *[He picks up rings and returns to throwing position]*

Mick: *[To BIRD]* 'Tis nothing these days but young married women guzzling gin and up till all hours playing bingo or jingo or whatever they call it. *[To MAGGIE]* You're a fine moral woman, ma'am. There's no one can deny that.

[MICK goes behind the counter and locates a large pad. He extracts spectacles from convenient case and rejoins MAGGIE at the table. His manner is now more efficient and business-like]

Mick: What kind of property do you wish to sell, Missus?

Maggie: 'Tis the four-acre field; the one you mentioned.

Mick: There's a great demand for land these days. The country is full of upstarts, on the make for grazing. No shortage of buyers. *[Has poured himself a drink. Puts jotter on counter]* Now ma'am, your full name and address. *[He readies his jotter and pencil]*

Maggie: Maggie Butler.

Mick: *[Writes laboriously]* Mrs Margaret Butler. And the address?

Maggie: Inchabawn, Carraigthomond.

Mick: *[Writing]* Inchabawn, Carraigthomond. I know that field well. The one over the river.

Maggie: That's the one . . . the only one.

[BIRD is now watching]

Mick: A handsome parcel of land. Fine inchy grazing and dry as a carpet. How do you hold it?

Maggie: What?

Mick: Your title? I mean, where's your title?

[MICK comes from behind counter, glancing at BIRD as he passes. Sits right of MAGGIE]

Mick: *[Kindly]* In other words, who gave you the right to sell it?

Maggie: 'Twas willed to me by my husband five years ago. 'Twas purchased under the Land Act by my husband's father, Patsy Butler. He willed it to my husband and my husband willed it to me. I'm the registered owner of the field.

Mick: That's fair enough for anything.

Bird: *[Closing in a bit]* I know that field. You let the grazing to the Bull McCabe.

Maggie: That's right. He has the grazing but only till the end of the month.

Mick: I fancy the Bull won't want to see it bought by an outsider. 'Tis bordering his own land.

[Look between BIRD and MICK. BIRD goes back to throw last ring or two]

Mick: And proper order, too. Well now, the acreage?

Maggie: Three acres one rood and thirty-two perches, bordering the river, with a passage to water and a passage to the main Carraigthomond road. 'Tis well fenced and there's a concrete stall in one corner near the river. There's two five-bar iron gates . . . and there's it's folio . . . 668420.

[BIRD finishes throwing rings, goes and gathers them together and hangs them on board. Then back to bar for rest of his drink]

Mick: And the valuation?

Maggie: Three pounds ten shillings, Poor Law.

Mick: Under fee simple, I take it?

Maggie: Fee simple.

Mick: Who's the solicitor, ma'am?

Maggie: Alfie Nesbitt.

Mick: No better man!

Bird: *[Who had been whistling sotto voce]* The Bull McCabe
                  won't like this!

Mick: You're telling me!

Maggie: Mr Flanagan, the highest bidder will get the field.

Mick: Oh that you may be sure. But the Bull is sure to be the
                  highest bidder. He needs that field. Well, Mrs Butler . . .
                  Maggie . . . I'll stick a notice in the paper this evening
                  and I'll have thirty-six bills printed and ready the day
                  after tomorrow.

Maggie: *[Gathering herself together and rising]* May God bless
                  you, Mr Flanagan.

Mick: It's my job, ma'am, it's my job. I suppose you'll have a
                  reserve?

Maggie: You'll put a reserve of £800 on it, Mr Flanagan.

Mick: That's more than £200 an acre!

Maggie: It's worth every penny of it. It's good land and it's well
                  situated.

Mick: True for you! True for you! You'll get the last brown
                  copper for it. I'll make sure of that.

Maggie: 'Tis all I have apart from my widow's pension and I can't
                  live on that. God will reward you if you get a good price
                  for me. *[She rises]* Is there money going to you?

Mick: No! No! That will come from the purchaser. Let me see
                  then, we'll make it the fifth of April.

Maggie: The fifth of April, please God. I'll see you then.

Mick: Please God is right and God is good, ma'am. God is good.

                  [MICK sees her to the door]

Maggie:	My husband always said you were an honest man, that I was to come to you if I was ever forced to sell. The Lord have mercy on him, he was a good honest man.
Mick:	He was, to be sure. A good kindly innocent man.
Maggie:	Good-day to you now.
Mick:	Good-day to you, ma'am.
	[Exit MAGGIE BUTLER]
Bird:	You've a nice tricky job facing you now.
Mick:	Don't I know it, but business is business, Bird, and business comes first with me.
Bird:	The Bull McCabe won't like it.
Mick:	What the Bull likes and don't like is nothing to me. I have my job to do.
	[Enter MAIMIE, MICK'S wife, who has come downstairs]
Maimie:	Bird.
Bird:	Maimie.
Maimie:	You're dinner is ready.
Mick:	Good. I'll go right up. Will you type out a couple of copies of this for me?
	[He hands her pages from jotter]
Maimie:	How many do you want?
Mick:	Make it three. Three should do. The Bird will carry one up to the printers when you're done.
Maimie:	Don't be too long . . . I'll be going to the hairdressers when you come down.
Mick:	Oh! What's on?
	[MICK stops]
Maimie:	*[Goes for typewriter behind bar]* Nothing's on, only that it's six weeks since I had my hair done.

Mick:	Why didn't you go and get it done before this? I don't like rushing my dinner. No one ever stopped you from getting your hair done.
Maimie:	No one . . . only nine kids. *[MICK glowers]* The baby's asleep, so you needn't turn on the wireless. If he wakes, that's the end of my hair-do.
Mick:	Cripes Almighty, woman, I want to hear the news.
Maimie:	Well, you can miss the news for one day.
Mick:	*[Turns again]* What's for dinner?
Maimie:	Corned beef and cabbage.
Mick:	Again?
Maimie:	What do you expect — turkey and ham?
Mick:	No, but God damn it, if I ate any more cabbage I'll have to put up a second lavatory.
	[Exit MICK]
Maimie:	*[Bringing typewriter to table and settling up to type — sitting]* No matter what you do, they aren't happy. What's for dinner, he asks. Ask him in the morning what he'd like for dinner and he'll tell you 'tis too soon after his breakfast.
Bird:	Put a half whiskey in that, will you?
Maimie:	Have you the price of it?
Bird:	No . . . but I'm selling two calves this evening.
Maimie:	Cash on the line only.
	[She inserts paper into typewriter]
Bird:	*[Rises and crosses with glass, drink not finished]* By God, you're an amazin' woman the way you keep up your appearance. I mean, after nine children, you're still the best-lookin' bird in Carraigthomond.
Maimie:	Come off it!
Bird:	'Twasn't me said that now, 'twas somebody else I'm quotin'. There was a bunch of us at the corner the other night and young Nesbitt started off about you. The way these young fellows talk about married women.

Maimie:	The solicitor's son?
Bird:	The very man! Just after you passed, he said 'there goes the finest-lookin' woman in the village'.
	[He finishes drink]
Maimie:	I'm not bad when I'm dressed up . . . if I had the time, that is. There's other good-looking women in Carraigthomond, you know.
Bird:	Sure, there are . . . but it was you young Nesbitt picked out. He ought to know and he almost a doctor.
	[Puts empty glass in front of her]
Maimie:	I don't know why I listen to you. *[She takes his glass and pours a half-whiskey into it]* Not a word about this and make sure you pay me when you have it.
Bird:	*[Follows to the bar]* Trust me! trust me!
Maimie:	He's not a bad looking chap.
Bird:	Who?
Maimie:	Young Nesbitt.
Bird:	Handsome, handsome.
Maimie:	What had he to say for himself?
Bird:	He never stopped talking for ten minutes. Couldn't figure out why you married your man.
Maimie:	I hadn't much sense at nineteen. Nine kids in a dump where you wouldn't get a chance to see yourself in a mirror. The drapers won't even put panties in the windows here — hypocrites. *[She starts to type. Pause]* Do you know what kills me, Bird? It's watching those sanctimonious bitches on their way to the altar of God every Sunday with their tongues out like bloody vipers for the body of Christ, and the host is hardly melted in their mouths when they're cuttin' the piss out of one another again!
Bird:	I don't know how you manage to look so good with all you have to do.

Maimie: *[As if she hadn't heard]* If you get your hair done different they whisper about you. Dress up in a bit of style and they stare at you. You'd want an armoured car if you wore a pair of slacks. Do you know how long it is since he had a bath? A year! Imagine, a whole year! He changes his shirt every Sunday and sleeps in it for the rest of the week.

[Typing]

Bird: Amazing! Amazing!

Maimie: The last time he wore a pyjamas was seventeen years ago . . . the night of our honeymoon.

Bird: How you stick it, I don't know.

[MAIMIE continues to type. She reads a sentence]

Maimie: '. . . an unfailing water supply with . . . *[She cannot make out the word at first]* access to the river.' Spell access?

Bird: A...X...I...S

[Enter 'THE BULL' McCABE followed by his son TADHG. BULL wears a hat and overcoat, carries an ashplant . . . TADHG is well-built and sour. He is in his twenties and wears a cap]

Bull: Was oul' Maggie Butler in here?

Maimie: She only just left.

Bird: How's the Bull?

Bull: Who gave you the right to call me Bull, you pratey-snappin' son-of-a-bitch.

Bird: Sorry Bull, sorry.

[Retreats to head of counter]

Bull: *[To MAIMIE]* Where's Mick? *[Peering at what she is typing]*

Maimie: Upstairs, finishing his dinner.

[She covers typing, picks up the lot and goes behind counter]

Bull: Two bottles of stout and sixpence worth o' them round biscuits.

[MAIMIE goes for order]

Tadhg: You. Hump off!

Bird: Sure, Tadhg, sure.

[BIRD swallows whiskey and is about to depart]

Bull: Wait a minute! Sit down here. *[Indicates table]* Have a drink?

Bird: *[Nervously]* A half whiskey.

Bull: Three bottles o' stout, Maimie. *[To TADHG]* What do you suppose?

Tadhg: I'd say he knows all. Wouldn't you know by the cut of him?

Bull: I'd say so, too. *[To BIRD]* She was puttin' up the field, wasn't she, Bird?

Bird: That's right! Fifth of April is the day, by public auction.

Bull: You have a good ear, Bird.

Bird: She made no secret of it.

Tadhg: You'd think she might have told us.

[BULL grunts, rises and fetches the three bottles of stout from bar to table, also the bag of biscuits. He pays and leaves his ashplant on stage, right of counter]

Bull: Will he be long?

Maimie: He shouldn't be too long.

[BULL returns to seat. He takes a sip of stout and eats a biscuit, as does TADHG]

Bull: *[To BIRD]* The fifth of April, you say?

Bird: That's it! I was here.

Bull: Did she put a price on it?

Bird: £800.

Bull: She's out of her mind!

Tadhg: A head case!

[MAIMIE types and finishes, pulls out paper from machine. Then sits behind counter and reads paper]

Bird: 'Tis a good bit of land though, Bull. You'll have to admit that.

Bull: Oh, I'll admit it all right but 'twas the manure of my heifers that made it good. Five years of the best cow-dung in Carraigthomond and £40 a year for grazing. That's £200 I paid her, not counting the cost of the cow-dung and the thistles we cut year in year out. To me, that field isn't worth a penny over £400. I reckon if she got £200 more from me she'd be well paid. Wouldn't you say so, Tadhg? . . . Bird, wouldn't you say so?

Bird: You're a fair man, Bull.

Bull: She'd be well paid indeed, if I was to fork out £200.
[BULL takes a drink]

Bird: Very well paid . . . but suppose there's other bidders, Bull?

Bull: *[Surprise]* There won't be any other bidders! I'll see to that. Half this village is related to me and them that isn't is related to my wife.

Bird: There's bound to be outsiders bidding. There's a craze for land everywhere.

[BULL points at his ashplant, which is near the counter, seizes it and strikes the floor with force. He brings drink with him and leans on counter]

Bull: That's what I care about outsiders. Accursed friggers with nothing in their heads only to own the ground we're walking on. We had their likes long enough, hadn't we? Land is all that matters, Tadhg boy, own your own land.

[BULL sits on stool, right end of bar]

Bird: You're right too, Bull. Dead right . . . Well, the wife will be wondering what's keepin' me. She'll have the dinner on the table by now.

[He rises to go]

Bull: You never ate a full dinner in your life and neither did your wife, you caffler, you! Whiskey is your dinner, supper and tea. How long since you ate an egg, you little rat, you, or a pound o' beef?

Bird:	*[Coming back]* Ah, now, she'll be worryin', Bull, an' you know what women are?
Bull:	Why wouldn't I? Haven't I one of my own, God bless her? *[Shouts]* Sit down. *[Shouts to MAIMIE]* What's he eatin' up there? *[BIRD sits]* A cow, is it?
Maimie:	He shouldn't be very long more.
Bull:	I suppose he's beginning his jelly and custard. That's good, Tadhg . . . jelly and custard. *[TADHG rises and goes to BULL. Has bag of biscuits. Finishes drink]*
Tadhg:	Da!
Bull:	*[Genuine affection]* Yes, Tadhg?
Tadhg:	We'll have to get this field.
Bull:	*[Squeezing TADHG's arm, taking bag of biscuits]* An' we'll get it, we'll get it, oul' stock. By all rights 'tis our property an' we're not men to be cheated out of our property. *[TADHG seizes a few biscuits. BULL downs his stout and examines his pocket-watch]*
Bull:	God, how I could frighten a feed of bacon and cabbage now, I guarantee you that. *[Shouts to MAIMIE]* Will he be long more?
Maimie:	I'll give him a call. *[She comes from behind counter and goes to stairway]*
Bull:	*[To TADHG and BIRD]* There's nothing like a Bull to move a heifer, hah!
Maimie:	Hurry on down, Mick, Mr McCabe want to see you. *[There is a muffled reply from MICK]*
Bull:	What did he say?
Maimie:	He's finishing his tea.
Bull:	His tea! Is it his supper or his dinner he's having? Tell him to bring his tea down with him and drink it here.

Maimie:	Bring your tea down with you. Mr McCabe is in a hurry. *[Shouting upstairs]*
Bull:	Tell him myself had no dinner yet nor had Tadhg.
	[TADHG gobbles a few more biscuits]
Maimie:	He says he'll be down in a minute. *[Make this line almost a gibe]* He has to go to the toilet.
	[She sits behind bar]
Bull:	O, Merciful father! He can't eat his dinner without going to the lavatory!
Bird:	I'll slip away . . . I'll come back again if you want me for anything.
Bull:	*[Peevishly]* Can't you sit still? 'Tis no wonder they call you after a bird. You're worse than a bloody sparrow!
Tadhg:	He's here!
	[Enter MICK]
Mick:	How're the men? How's Bull, how are you? And Tadhg, how're you?
Bull:	We hadn't our dinner yet and the two of us fasting since morning.
Mick:	What can I do for you?
Bull:	*[Indicates MAIMIE]* 'Tis private.
Mick:	*[To MAIMIE]* Are you goin' to the hairdresser?
	[MAIMIE operates cash register and extracts a note. She exits without a word. As she is going off, BULL blows up the biscuit bag and bursts it]
Mick:	Well, now, what's the problem?
Bull:	The Bird here tells me you have a field for sale.
Mick:	That's right!
Bull:	You're aware of the fact that me and Tadhg has had the grazing of this field for the past five years and has the grazin' of it now?

Mick:	Yes, I am. Of course I am.
Bull:	Five times £40 is £200. A lot of money!
Mick:	'Tis a lot!
Bull:	I'll grant you 'tis a lot. A lot of countin' in hard-earned single pound notes.

[BIRD looks at BULL knowing what's coming]

Bull:	£200 in grazing alone. Who'd pay it but myself.
Mick:	Five forties is a fair sum.
Bull:	'Twould give me as much claim to the field as the woman who has it for sale.

[MICK doesn't answer]

Tadhg:	There wouldn't be a stitch of grass in it only for the manure of the heifers . . . our heifers!
Bull:	And the bullocks! Don't forget the bullocks, Tadhg. Our bullocks is more fat and content than women with husbands in England.
Tadhg:	'Twas us that kept the donkeys out of it.
Bull:	Donkeys! If there's one thing that addles me, it's wandering donkeys. I can't sleep at night over them. I swear to you I get into bed happy and there I'd be just settling down when I'd think of the long-eared thievin' pirates. No sleep for me that night. I keep thinking of the grass they eat on me, and the clover . . . the fine young clover.
Tadhg:	A hungry ass would eat as much as two cows.
Bull:	If he's an ass, he's after grass — someone else's grass. I often come across a lonesome ass in April when you'd see no growth anywhere an' you'd be sparin' the young fields for hungry heifers. Like the black stallion donkey with the single ear and the eyes like a saint?
Tadhg:	Oh, Christ!
Bull:	The first time I met that bastard was a Stephen's Day and he staring through one of the gates of the field we're buying now. You'd think butter wouldn't melt in his

mouth. To look at his face you'd think grass was the last thing in his head. He gave me a look and he trotted off. That night he broke the gate. Three months we watched him till we cornered him. Tadhg there beat him to death. He was a solid hour flaking him with his fists and me with a blackthorn . . . An' do you mean to tell me I have no claim to that field? That any outside stranger can make his open bid and do us out of what's ours, after we huntin' every connivin' jackass from the countryside?

Mick: Ah, now, Bull, be fair, she's entitled to the best price she can get. The field is legally hers.

Bull: An' she'll get a fair price. I'll hand you over £200 here an' now an' you'll give me a receipt.

Mick: £200! Ah, you'll have to do better than that. Anyway, 'tis for public auction on these premises, the fifth of April. 'Tis out of my hands, Bull . . . Sorry!

Bull: Is the bills out yet for it?

Mick: No, not yet.

Bull: Did you notify the papers?

Mick: I'm just on the point of doing it.

[Lifting MAIMIE'S typing]

Bull: *[Pointing to it]* On the point of it, but 'tisn't done.

Tadhg: If it goes to the papers, you'll have twenty bidding for it.

Bull: We can't have that. *[Pause. Hand on typing . . .]* And we won't have that.

Mick: *[Detaches papers from BULL'S hand]* The auction will have to be held.

Bull: And let it be held! There will be no one here but ourselves.

Mick: Ah, now, you know well there will be more than you interested. That's a good bit of land.

Bull: If it don't go to the papers an' if there's no bills who's going to know except what's here?

Mick:	You can't do that!
Bull:	'Twas done before. You did it yourself.
Mick:	This is different. Old Nesbitt, the solicitor, knows about this.
Bull:	He's an old crook and, if you ask me, he won't be here the day of the auction.
Mick:	What are you going to do? Kidnap him?
Bull:	There's a few old granduncles of mine with wills to be made. One of them could be dying that day, couldn't he? Oul' Nesbitt wouldn't want to fall out with our clan.
Mick:	Hold it! Hold it! I can't be a party to this. There's a reserve of £800 and the old woman needs the money. Besides, it's illegal.
Bull:	*[Laughs]* Illegal! That's a good one! *[Nudges his companions]* Did you hear that . . . illegal?
Mick:	There's my commission. Five percent of £800 is £40. I'm not going to lose £40 because you need a cheap field.
Bull:	*[Threateningly]* I need that field! I have nineteen acres and no passage to water. I have to get a passage. I'll pay you the £40 the day of the auction, provided my bid is accepted.
Mick:	I'd like to see that in writing.
Bull:	Writing? . . . Do you want me to be hanged? I'll sign nothing. Look! You needn't sign over the field 'till I plank the £40 into the palm of your hand.
Tadhg:	That's fair enough for anything, isn't it, Bird?
Bird:	'Tis reasonable.
Bull:	There will be something for Bird, too. We won't forget the Bird.
Mick:	You don't seem to understand that this is highway robbery.
Bull:	'Tis worse robbery the other way. Do you want some hangblasted shagger of a stranger to get it?

Mick: What about Maggie Butler? 'Tis her field and no one else's.

Bull: 'Tis as much mine! Look here, Flanagan, there's nothing to prevent a boycott of your shop.

Mick: What . . . what do you mean?

Bull: There's a hundred relations of mine in this village and around it. Not one of them will ever set foot in this pub again if I say so.

Mick: Give me the £40 now and I'll do my best.

[BULL laughs and TADHG moves to his left shoulder]

Bull: I'll give you the half of it. I'll give you £20 the day of the sale. Fair enough?

Mick: Fair enough! The Bird better keep his trap shut.

Bull: The Bird don't like to get his feathers wet. Do you, Bird? There's many a deep hole in the river below and who's to say how a man might lose his footing?

Bird: My lips are sealed.

[BULL draws a wallet from his pocket and extracts two tenners]

Bull: *[To MICK]* Here's two ten pound notes. The Bird here will act as a witness. Put your hand here, Bird, *[He places BIRD'S hand over MICK'S]* and say after me *[Authoritative tone]* . . . As God is my judge . . .

Bird: As God is my judge . . .

Bull: I swear by my solemn oath . . .

Bird: I swear by my solemn oath . . .

Bull: That I witness the receipt of £20 by Mick Flanagan . . .

Bird: That I witness the receipt of £20 by Mick Flanagan . . .

Bull: Of the first part . . .

Bird: Of the first part . . .

Bull: From the person of Thady McCabe of the second part . . .

Bird: From the person of Thady McCabe of the second part . . .

Bull:	*[Proudly with grim humour]* Here-in-after, affectionately known as the Bull . . I'm no fool when it comes to law, boys.
Tadhg:	Hear! Hear!
Bull:	I'm as big a rogue as any solicitor.
Mick:	I'll have to get the bills printed but I'll get the lot burned when they come from the printers.
Bull:	Solid thinking . . . very solid! Now, here's what we'll do. The morning of the auction the Bird here opens the bidding with a £100 and I rise him £10. *[Increasing in tempo]* The Bird goes to £120 and again I rise him £10. The Bird soars up to £150 and again I rise him £10. The Bird flies higher to £190 but I'm there with the final bid of £200. All straight and fair and above board. Two down, as the man said, and carry one. What about the printer? Is he trustable?
Mick:	Safer than a confession.
Bird:	What about me, Bull?
Bull:	What about you?
Bird:	You promised me something.
Bull:	What would you say to £5?
Bird:	I'll take it.
Bull:	The minute the land changes hands, 'tis yours.
Bird:	What about a £1 on deposit?
Bull:	*[Wounded]* Is it how you don't trust me?
Bird:	No . . . No . . . Good God, no!
Bull:	You won't be forgot, Bird. You have my guarantees on that.
Bird:	Stand us a half-one before you go?
Bull:	Give him a half-one, Mick. We'll all have one. Have one yourself, Mick.

[BULL throws coin on counter and MICK goes to fetch

whiskey]

Bull: *[Leaning on bar, in an ecstasy of accomplishment]*
I watched this field for forty years and my father before
me watched it for forty more. I know every rib of grass
and every thistle and every whitethorn bush that bounds
it. *[To BIRD]* There's shamrock in the south-west corner.
Shamrock, imagine! The north part is bound by forty sloe
bushes. Some fool planted them once, but they're a good
hedge. This is a sweet little field, this is an independent
little field that wants eatin'.

Bird: Well, you'll have it soon *[Accepts whiskey from MICK]* with
the help of God.

Bull: *[Looks at him suspiciously for a moment but goes on]*
When oul' Maggie's husband died five years ago, I knew
he was dying. One look at the writin' under his eyes and
I knew. I knew the wife was feeling the pinch lately. I knew
by the writin'. 'Twas wrote as plain as a process across her
forehead and in the wrinkles of her cheeks. She was feelin'
the pinch of hunger. *[Suddenly to BIRD who becomes trans-
fixed]* Bird, I swear to you that I could tell what a man be
thinking by the writin' on his face.

Bird: Have no fear o' me!

Bull: *[Affable]* I won't oul' stock, for I know you're to be trusted
above any man I know.

Tadhg: Da, what about the dinner?

Bull: *[Proudly]* There's your healthy man! When he isn't hungry
for women, he's hungry for meat. Tadhg, my son, marry
no woman if she hasn't land.

[Enter a youngish sergeant of civic guards in full uniform]

Sergeant: Good afternoon, men!

Mick: Ah, good afternoon to you, Sergeant Leahy. Would you
care for a drink?

Sergeant: Thank you, no, Mick.

Bull: *[To TADHG]* Come on away or our dinner will be perished.

Sergeant: I didn't call to see you, Mick. I came to have a word with

Mr McCabe here.

Bull:	Well, you'll have to postpone it because I'm going to my dinner.
Sergeant:	This won't take long. I'm here investigating the death of a donkey.

[Laughter from all]

Bull:	Investigating the death of an ass! You wouldn't hear it in a play! By gor! 'Tis the same law the whole time. The same dirty English law. No change at all.
Sergeant:	Maybe not, but I have to ask your son and yourself a few questions.
Bull:	You're out of your mind, Sergeant. Come on away home, Tadhg. God, have ye anything else to do? What about all the murders and the robberies? 'Twould be more in your line to be solving them. Come on, Tadhg, this fellow is like all the rest of 'em. His brains are in the arse of his trousers.
Sergeant:	*[Sharply]* That's enough of that! Sit down and answer my questions . . . sit down or come to the Barracks!
Bull:	Sit down, Tadhg . . . *[Smugly]* There's more thought of donkeys in this world than there is of Christians.
Sergeant:	Where were you the night before last?
Bull:	What night was that?
Sergeant:	*[To TADHG]* Where were you last night?
Tadhg:	Where's that we were again, da?
Bull:	We were at home playing cards.
Sergeant:	Until what time?
Bull:	Till morning.
Sergeant:	And did you leave the house during that time?
Bull:	We were in the backyard a few times, or is that ag'in the law, too?
Sergeant:	Can you prove that you didn't visit Mrs Butler's field over

the river on that night?

Bull: On my solemn oath and conscience, if we left the house for more than two minutes.

Sergeant: You have that field taken for grazing, haven't you?

Bull: Everyone knows that.

Sergeant: Well, can you prove you weren't there?

Bull: The Bird there was playing cards with us till two o' clock in the mornin'.

Sergeant: Is that the truth, Bird?

Bird: Gospel!

Sergeant: Well, the donkey was killed around midnight. His cries were heard by a couple walking along the river. They reported to the SPCA who in turn reported it to the Barrack Orderly. What I want to know is where were ye when the donkey was poisoned?

Tadhg: He wasn't poisoned!

Sergeant: How do you know he wasn't poisoned?

Tadhg: Well . . .

Bull: Because there's no poison on our lands. That's how he knows an' don't be doin' the smart man with your tricky questions. What is he but an innocent boy that never told a lie in his whole life. You don't care, do you, so long as you can get a conviction. Tell me, where do you disappear to when there's tinkers fightin', an' law-abidin' men gettin' stabbed to death in the street?

Sergeant: Bird, you say you were at this man's house that night and I say — you're a liar!

Bird: Ye all heard it! Ye all heard what he said! You called me a liar, Sergeant, and no man does that to the Bird O'Donnell. No man — uniform or no uniform.

Sergeant: All right! All right! I take it back. I apologise for calling you a liar.

Bird: You better not do it again! *[Somewhat mollified]*

Sergeant: I'm wasting my time! There's nothing in your heads but pigs and cows and pitiful patches of land. You laugh when you hear that an old jackass was beaten to death, but a man might be beaten to death here for all you'd give a damn.

[Exit SERGEANT LEAHY]

Bull: And a Sergeant might get his face split open one night and all the guards in Ireland wouldn't find out who did it . . . not if they searched till Kingdom Come!

Scene 2

[Action takes place as before.
The time is the morning of April the fifth. MAIMIE FLANAGAN is behind the bar. Three of the children are playing in and around the bar area. The BIRD is seated at table with a glass of whiskey in front of him. The BIRD rises and approaches the counter. He brings his whiskey along with him and swallows it at the counter. He places glass on counter and takes coin from his pocket which he places on the counter]

Maimie: Good girl, Nellie, will you go upstairs and look after the baby?

Bird: Throw a drop of whiskey into that, will you? *[He carefully arranges money on the counter]* Just enough!

[Enter boys from the street]

Bird: Close the bloody door, I'm perished.

[MAIMIE pours whiskey, takes money and places it in cash register]

Maimie: *[To boys]* Upstairs!

Bird: I see you got your hair done.

Maimie: About time, wasn't it?

Bird: It suits you. *[Surveys it from an angle]* Definitely suits you. Kind of a girly look.

Maimie: *[Touches her hair up]* D'you think so? 'Tis the latest . . . well, the latest around here anyway . . .

[Enter LEAMY with a box of stout]

Leamy: My father said you were short of stout.

Maimie: Thanks, Leamy. What's he doin' up there?

Leamy: Listenin' to the wireless. The baby's crying, Muddy.
               What'll I do with him?

Maimie: Give him a suck out of the bottle and if he doesn't settle
               down, call me, Leamy.

Leamy: All right, Muddy.

Maimie: Aoife, take Mary upstairs. Leamy, take this fellow upstairs,
               there's an auction going on here this morning.

Leamy: *[To BIRD who is now throwing rings]* Bird, you'd hook a
               farmer quicker than you'd hook a thirteen.

               [Exit LEAMY, mock-chased by BIRD]

Maimie: Well, did he like it?

Bird: What?

Maimie: Me hair.

Bird: Who?

Maimie: The fellow you told me about. Young Nesbitt, the
               solicitor's son.

Bird: Oh, he was on about you again the other night.

Maimie: What did he say?

Bird: How did a good-looking woman like Maimie Flanagan get
               stuck in a dump like this? That's what he said . . . how did
               she get stuck in a dump like this?

Maimie: Stuck is right! He seems like a nice young fellow. Why don't
               you bring him in for a drink sometime? Or does he drink?

Bird: Does he what? He doesn't drink around here, though . . .
               too much talk. You can't blame him. You know what
               they're like around here?

Maimie: You're right there! You couldn't turn in your bed but
               they'd know it.

Bird: There's a lot of jealousy. It must be a holy terror to be a
               good-lookin' woman an' all them oul' frowsies gabbin'
               about you. An 'tis worse if you're not appreciated by
               them who should appreciate you.

Maimie: Sure, even if I talk to any good-looking fella in the bar,
               himself does be mad jealous. You'd think I was goin' to
               run away with one of 'em.

Bird: No one but yourself would stick it. You've got the
               patience of Job.

Maimie: Oh, he can be terrible. D'you remember the time last year
               I went to the dance in town . . . that I thought he'd be
               spending the night in Dublin?

Bird: You looked good that night. Mind you, I wasn't the only
               one who remarked it.

Maimie: Four years since I was at a dance, and imagine. . . . on
               that one night he should get a lift home unexpectedly!

Bird: *[Gets off stool and comes to her]* What did he do?

Maimie: Waited up till I came home. I asked a few of the boys in
               for a drink and he hiding all the time around in the stairway.
               [The BIRD whistles] Heard every word we said. Luck o' God,
               'twas all innocent. He got a great suck-in. It's a pity I
               didn't know he was listening I'd have stuck in something
               deliberately.

Bird: A pity!

Maimie: 'Twould have been great gas if we all knelt down and said
               the Rosary.

Bird: But what happened? What happened?

Maimie: Oh, he waited till the boys were gone and there he was,
               sitting on the steps of the stairs as I was going up. Christ,
               I thought I'd drop dead . . . he struck me and I fell down
               the stairs. I pretended to be unconscious. That frightened
               him. You should have heard him! Oh, the lamenting would

	bring a laugh from a corpse.
Bird:	Good! . . . Good! . . . Go on!
Maimie:	'Wake up, Maim. Wake up, my little darling!' he never called me darling before, not even when we were courting. He got a bit annoyed then. 'Wake up, Maimie! will you wake up, in the name o' God, and don't disgrace me by being dead . . .'
Bird:	This is marvellous! . . . marvellous! . . .
Maimie:	Wait till you hear! 'Wake up,' said he and he started sobbing. 'Wake up, you bloody bitch. You want to have me hanged!' *[Both laugh]* He said the Act of Contrition into my ear after that and rushed over for the doctor and the priest. I had a brandy while I was waiting.
Bird:	Ah, this is priceless! . . .
Maimie:	Bird, were you ever anointed? *[BIRD looks askance at her]* Oh, it's a great sensation when you aren't sick . . . more soothing than getting your hair done . . . something like a massage . . . *[At this stage a newcomer enters and nods both to MAIMIE and the BIRD. He is a young man in his late twenties, well-dressed and presentable. He is WILLIAM DEE]*
Maimie:	Good morning.
William:	Good morning.
Bird:	Good morning.
Maimie:	Nice morning, isn't it?
William:	Yes, it is. Could I have a bottle of beer, please?
Bird:	'Tis inclined to be a bit showery, but all in all, 'tisn't bad for the time of year.
William:	April is a tricky month all right. You never know where you are with it.
Bird:	Like a woman!
William:	*[Considers this observation]* Yes, in some ways . . . Yes, it is! It's a strange month.

Bird: Fine one minute and wet the next. *[Playing with his glass]* I hate windy weather. I'm told there's good growth though. Should please the farmers.

William: A very difficult thing to do.

Bird: You aren't far wrong there. *[Sarcastically]* Still, they had a hard winter and they deserve a bit of comfort, the creatures!

Maimie: *[Placing drink on the counter]* Now, there you are!

[WILLIAM places money on the counter]

Bird: Good luck! *[Finishing drink ostentatiously]*

William: Would you care for a drink, sir?

Bird: Yes, indeed . . . a large whiskey, Maimie, please.

[MAIMIE fills the BIRD's glass and takes the price of it from WILLIAM's change]

Maimie: You're a stranger to these parts.

William: My wife was born around here. So I'm not a stranger . . . not a complete stranger, that is.

Maimie: Where was your wife born?

William: About six miles away . . . a place called Tubber.

Maimie: What was her name?

William: Connolly.

Bird: *[Thoughtfully]* Connolly! . . . Connolly! . . .

Maimie: I can't seem to place her.

Bird: Neither can I.

William: Well, that would be pretty hard for you. There's nobody of that name in Tubber now. The whole family moved to England twenty years ago.

Maimie: And are you from around here?

William: No. I'm a Galway man. I live in England. Living there twelve years. Me, if I had my way, that's where I'd like to stay.

Maimie: Is your wife with you?

William: No . . . she's in England. She may be joining me soon. It all depends.

Maimie: You're on holiday?

William: No . . . business. That's why I'm here. I came to see your husband. If he's around I'd like a few words with him.

Maimie: He's finishing his breakfast. I'll slip up and get him if you like. It's no trouble.

William: No, there's no hurry. Will you have a drink? I should have asked you in the first place.

Maimie: I don't know that I should!

Bird: Go on, for God's sake! You'll only be young once. *[To WILLIAM]* This is our local beauty queen.

Maimie: Don't mind him! . . . 'Twill have to be quick.

Bird: We won't tell . . . cross our hearts!

Maimie: I'll have a drop of brandy, so.

[WILLIAM places money on counter]

Bird: A gay soul, this one, as game as any.

Maimie: Here's cheers!

Bird: Good luck!

Maimie: *[Tosses back her drink quickly]* Now you'll have to have one on me.

William: Not for me, thanks. Too early!

[BIRD swallows his drink quickly and proffers his glass]

Bird: I won't say no, Maimie.

Maimie: It has to be a small one this time. We don't want him drunk, do we, Mister . . . ?

William: The name is Dee . . . William Dee.

Maimie: Mr Dee, are you sure you won't have one?

William: No, if you don't mind. Some other time, maybe. I'll be

here for a few days *[Sits on chair at table]* and it's possible
I'll be here permanently.

*[MAIMIE fills BIRD's drink and hands it to him. Takes
WILLIAM's money, gets change and gives it to him]*

William: Your husband is Michael Flanagan, the auctioneer, isn't he?

Maimie: That's right! I'll slip up and get him. *[Suggestively to DEE]*
Drop in again, some time, any time . . . Bird.

Bird: Maimie!

[Exit MAIMIE]

William: Seems like a nice woman.

Bird: You needn't say this to anyone . . . but she's a regular flier,
that one. Thirty, thirty.

William: *[Somewhat coldly]* She struck me as being a nice friendly
woman.

Bird: Ah, I was only having a bit of a joke. You're right about
her, though. She's lovely.

[MICK appears at stairway]

Mick: Good morning, gentlemen! *[To WILLIAM]* The wife tells me
you were wanting to see me.

William: I'm sorry if I disturbed you. There's no particular hurry.

Mick: That's all right. I was only listening to the late news . . .
What can I do for you?

William: Well, first of all, let me introduce myself. My name is
William Dee.

Mick: I'm Mick Flanagan. *[He shakes hands with WILLIAM]*
How do you do?

William: I have a letter here from Mr Nesbitt, the solicitor, about the
sale of a field. *[Looks at watch]* The auction was supposed
to take place at eleven o' clock today. Maybe, there's been
a mistake . . .

Mick: No, there's no mistake. This is the day of the auction, all
right. But who told you? How did you get in touch with
oul' Nesbitt?

William:	It's the wife, you see. Since our last baby her nerves haven't been too good and she wants to come back to Ireland. Mr Nesbitt was one of the many solicitors I wrote to, to be on the lookout for just such a field. Last week I had a letter from him so I took a chance and came over. Sláinte!

[MICK picks up WILLIAM's empty glass and goes and fills half-pint]

Mick:	You may have come on a fool's errand.

[MICK gives the beck to the BIRD who finishes his drink and exits quickly]

William:	I don't understand.
Mick:	There's only four acres . . . you couldn't possibly make a living there.
William:	I'm not worried about that. My site in England is much less.
Mick:	Don't get me wrong now, my friend. I'm only advising you for your own good.
William:	I've a business of my own in England and I do fairly well. I supply concrete blocks to builders. This field is the right size for me. It's on a river with first-class gravel.
Mick:	Who told you? About the gravel, I mean?
William:	I had an engineer from the town look it over.
Mick:	An engineer! That must have been the fellow with the wooden box. Said he was catching eel fry . . . You'd want a fortune to start a business like that!
William:	It's not as difficult as it sounds. I cover an acre or so with concrete, move in my machinery and I'm in business.
Mick:	*[Putting free drink before WILLIAM]* It's only fair to tell you there's a boycott on outside bidders.
William:	Nesbitt said nothing about a boycott.
Mick:	Well, that's the way it is. There's a boycott all right and there could be trouble . . . serious trouble.
William:	What sort of boycott?

Mick: I wouldn't want to lead you astray but for the past five years now a farmer whose land is right next to the field has rented the grazing. He believes he has first claim . . .

William: It's a public auction, isn't it?

Mick: Yes . . . yes . . . but I thought I'd warn you. The village would hold it against you.

William: I wouldn't be selling blocks to the village.

Mick: You wouldn't get men to work for you.

William: A few of my men in England would give their right hands to get back to Ireland.

Mick: You don't know about land. You're a stranger . . . you wouldn't understand. There will be trouble.

William: All I know is that my wife isn't well. If I don't get her back here quick, she'll crack up. Now, if that isn't trouble, tell me, what is?

Mick: Look! I'll tell you what . . . you go back to your wife and I'll find a suitable field for you. I won't let you down. I'll search high and low. You won't have long to wait.

William: You're an auctioneer?

Mick: Yes.

William: And this is a public auction?

Mick: Yes.

William: Well, I'm a prospective buyer, so how about getting along with the auction?

[Enter MAIMIE with a tea-tray. She comes between them]

Maimie: *[To WILLIAM]* Would you like a cup of tea?

[MICK glowers at MAIMIE as she places tea on table]

William: Thanks, I would.

Mick: D'you know what he's doin'?

Maimie: No . . . what?

Mick: He's biddin' for the field!

Maimie:	What's so awful about that?
Mick:	*[Furious]* Cripes Almighty, woman!

[MAIMIE exits with the tea-tray]

William:	I'm not so welcome, am I?
Mick:	Look, I've nothing against you personally.
William:	And I've nothing against you, personally or otherwise.

[Enter MAGGIE BUTLER]

Mick:	Ah, there you are, Mrs Butler. You're welcome!
Maggie:	Is it time for the auction yet?
Mick:	Any minute now. We're waiting for the bidders.
Maggie:	There don't seem to be many here.
Mick:	It won't be so. It won't be so, I assure you.

[Enter MAIMIE]

William:	*[To MAGGIE]* Are you the owner of the field?
Maggie:	I am, sir.
William:	I'm pleased to meet you. My name is Dee . . . William Dee. I expect to be bidding for your property . . .
Mick:	*[Confidentially to MAGGIE]* It might be better if you weren't here until the auction starts. Why don't you go upstairs with Maimie for a cup of tea?
Maimie:	Aye, Maggie, do.
Maggie:	Very well. *[She rises and MAIMIE solicitously takes charge of her]* You'll do your best for me, Mr Flanagan?
Mick:	We'll do our best, our very best.
Maggie:	You'll be sure to call me, Mr Flanagan.
Mick:	To be sure, to be sure.
Maimie:	Come on this way, Maggie, watch the toys.

[Exit MAGGIE and MAIMIE]

William:	As a prospective buyer, I have a right to know everything

about the field.

Mick: You know too bloody much!

William: I know how to look after myself.

[Enter the BIRD. He sidles to counter and rests his elbows on it, watching MICK and WILLIAM. He is followed almost immediately by the BULL McCABE who carries an ashplant. Following the BULL, comes his son, TADHG. They both glare at WILLIAM who is somewhat surprised by their attitude]

Bull: *[Stops inside door to survey WILLIAM]* Give us three half pints o' porter.

William: Hello there.

[MICK goes behind counter to draw the stout. The BULL scowls at WILLIAM who is somewhat amused by his antics]

Bull: We were told about you. Are you aware there's an objection here?

William: So I'm told.

Bull: What do you want the field for?

William: That's no business of yours.

Mick: He's going to make concrete blocks.

Bull: What?

Mick: To cover the field with concrete.

Bull: What about the grass? What about my lovely heifers?

Tadhg: No more meadows nor hay? *[To WILLIAM]* You're an oily son-of-a-bitch!

Bull: No foreign cock with hair-oil and a tie-pin is goin' to do me out of my rights. I've had that field for five years. It's my only passage to water. You're tacklin' a crowd now that could do for you, man. Watch out for yourself.

[MICK arrives with three bottles of stout]

Bull: Give us sixpence worth of biscuits — far-to-go ones.

William: *[To MICK]* Isn't it time the auction was started?

Bull:	If you know what's good for you, you won't bid.
William:	Is that a threat?
Tadhg:	*[Intimidating]* Make what you like of it!
William:	If you care to make youself clear, I certainly will
Tadhg:	*[Fighting pose]* If you fancy yourself, you can have it here.
William:	For God's sake, be your age!

[WILLIAM rises, goes to stairway and calls for MAGGIE BUTLER before anybody can stop him]

William: *[To others]* I think you'll all agree that Mrs Butler should be present. She *is* the rightful owner, I believe.

Mick: Mrs Butler, I'm going to start the auction now.

[MICK places bag of biscuits on table and accepts money from BULL]

Bull: *[To MICK]* He'll get his head split if he isn't careful. Bloody imported whoresmaster, taking over the village as if he owned it.

Mick: I want no trouble here now, Bull. There's a way for circumventing everything.

Bull: I'll circumvent him, if there's circumventing to be done.

[Enter MAGGIE BUTLER followed by MAIMIE]

Mick: Mrs Butler, take a seat.

[Reluctantly MICK goes behind counter and emerges with two long slips of white paper]

Mick: I'll read the conditions of sale. *[Stands on a low box]* The highest bidder shall be the purchaser and if any dispute arises as to any bidding, the property shall be put up again at the last undisputed bidding. There will be a reserve price and the vendor and her agents will be at liberty to bid. No person shall advance less than five pounds at any bidding and no bidding shall be retracted . . .

Bull: I see the dirty hand of the law in this!

Mick: *[Reading]* 'Two . . . The purchaser shall immediately on being declared as such, pay to the Auctioneer one-fourth of the purchase money as a deposit together with the usual auction fees of five per cent . . .' And so on and so forth, et cetera, et cetera.

[MICK hands form to MAIMIE who places it on counter. BULL snatches the paper]

Bull: Law! Law! *[To TADHG]* that's the dear material. All the money in Carraigthomond wouldn't pay for a suit length of that cloth.

[He slams form back on counter]

Mick: And now the 'Particulars and Conditions of Sale' . . . *[Reads from second paper]* 'Particulars and Conditons of Sale by Auction of the undermentioned property pursuant to advertisement duly published for the purpose . . .'

Bull: Oh, merciful God, that's the rigmarole. Start the bidding and get it over.

Mick: *[Hands paper to MAIMIE]* . . . Now, this land, as you all know, is well watered and well fenced with a carrying power of seven cattle . . .

Bull: Thanks to me and Tadhg. 'Twas our sweat that fenced it and our dung that manured it. Come on, man, get on with the bidding!

Mick: Do I hear an opening bid for this excellent property?

[BULL, TADHG and the BIRD sip their stout and nothing is to be heard unless it is the sound of TADHG crunching biscuits]

Mick: I repeat, ladies and gentlemen, will someone bid me for this fine field on the banks of the Oinseach river. *[Pause]* This property of three acres one rood and thirty two perches or thereabouts. This green grassy pasture . . . *[Pause]* . . . come on now! . . . Do I hear an opening bid? . . . Will someone bid me, please!

[BULL nods at the BIRD and the BIRD shuffles a pace forward]

Mick: Do I hear a bid?

Bird: £100

Mick: I hear you loud and clear, sir. £100 it is from the Bird O'Donnell . . . Now, this is more like it. Do I hear any advance on £100.

[All eyes are turned on WILLIAM *who calmly lights a cigarette]*

Bull: £110.

Mick: £110 from Mr Thady McCabe.

Bird: £120

Mick: £120 from Mr Bird O'Donnell.

Bull: £130.

Mick: Do I hear . . . Do I hear an increase on £130? Do I hear an increase on £130?

Bird: £150.

Mick: £150. Do I hear — ?

Bull: £160.

Mick: £160 from the Bull McCabe. Do I hear any advance on £160?

[At this stage they all look at WILLIAM *who smokes on unperturbed]*

Bird: £190.

Mick: Any advance on £190? Any advance on £190?

Bull: £200!

[Pause]

Mick: I have £200. Do I have any advance on £200? On £200? I have £200 from Mr Thady McCabe of Inchabawn . . . *[Again* WILLIAM *is the subject of all eyes]* Is this to be the final bid? There is a reserve and I will negotiate by private treaty with the highest bidder. C'mon now, ladies and gentlemen. Before I close this public auction, do I hear any advance on £200?

William: *[Casually]* Guineas!

Mick: Any advance on £200?

William: Two hundred guineas.

Tadhg: What's guineas?

Bull: He should be disqualified. There's no such thing as a guinea going these days.

William: All right. I'll bid £300.

[An audible hush]

Mick: *[Nervously]* I have £300 . . . have I any advance on £300? I'm bid £300. Do I hear £350? Do I hear £350? No! . . . In that event, I'll call a recess for a day and negotiate by private treaty.

[MICK is about to turn away but WILLIAM rises and stops him]

William: What time do you propose to start tomorrow?

Mick: Oh, some time in the morning. We can't all be on the dot like you. These people here are hardworking people with little time to spare.

William: What guarantee have I that you won't close the deal with him? *[Indicating BULL]*

Mick: Now, let that be the least of your worries. Everything is nice and legal here.

William: I take it then that my bid being the highest, you'll give me something in writing until morning.

Mick: *[Anger]* You'll get no bloody writing from me . . . You'll be here in the morning if you want to bid again.

William: Bid against whom?

Mick: *[For the benefit of MAGGIE BUTLER]* You'll bid till this woman's reserve has been reached. There's no one going to wrong an old woman, not while I'm on my feet, Mister. I'll give you a guarantee of that.

William: How much is the reserve?

Mick: £800.

William: That's not beyond me and I'm prepared to bid again.

When can I see the field?

[TADHG and BULL step forward]

Tadhg: Stay away from that field.

Bull: There's cattle of ours there.

William: If the field is for auction, I'm entitled to have a look at it.

Bull: Use your head while you're able. Stay away!

Tadhg: That's right! Get the hell out of here now . . . while you can.

Maggie: You can see my field any time, sir.

Bull: *[Roars]* Shut up, you oul' fool! What about my claim?

Maggie: You've no claim!

Bull: *[Dangerously]* Look out for youself, you! Look out for youself. *[He cows the old woman]*

William: I'll be back when you open in the morning.

Bull: That field is mine! Remember that! I'll pay a fair price. God Almighty! 'Tis a sin to cover grass and clover with concrete.

[MAGGIE BUTLER rises and moves towards doorway]

Maggie: *[To MAIMIE]* I'll have to be goin'. There's no one in the house but myself.

Bull: You should remember that!

[MAGGIE looks back, startled. WILLIAM acknowledges MAGGIE'S exit]

Bull: *[To WILLIAM]* Get out while you're clean!

William: I'll be back in the morning . . . and this time I'll be with my solicitor.

[WILLIAM exiting]

Bull: You might be back with more than your solicitor.

[WILLIAM exits. BULL, TADHG and MICK go into a huddle at the counter. The lights fade]

[Action takes place in the pub late that evening. LEAMY is at the door looking out MAIMIE is outside bar, watching him]

Maimie: *[To LEAMY after opening pause]* It's quiet, Leamy. You could have gone out with the boys.

Leamy: I'd rather be here with you, Muddy. You go out for a walk and I'll be OK. There won't be anybody in for a while.

Maimie: A funny thing, Mister, I'd rather be here with you, too. Give my back a rub like a good boy. *[LEAMY does so]* Oh, that's lovely!

Leamy: I wish it was always like this.

Maimie: Sit down, Leamy, and we'll treat ourselves to a drink.

Leamy: You stay there and I'll get it. *[He seats his mother]* Now, what'll it be? The sky's the limit!

Maimie: I'll have a drop of brandy. Are they asleep upstairs?

Leamy: All sound! . . . A small brandy it'll be.

[He goes behind counter]

Maimie: I haven't sat down since morning. It's like a holiday having a stretch. *[She yawns]* I wonder what it's like to have a job that ends at six with Saturdays and Sundays free and holidays. Can you imagine, Leamy . . . holidays. Sure, if we had holidays we wouldn't know what to do with 'em.

Leamy: *[Places drink on table and sits down]* Would you like a cigarette?

Maimie: Aye, they're over there by the register. You're a great boy! *[Lifts her glass]* Long life, Leamy!

Leamy: And the same to you, Muddy! *[They drink]* Do you feel it, too?

Maimie: Feel what?

Leamy: The fear! I'm getting afraid already. I'll bolt the door and put up the shutters and let nobody in. Let's just sit here and never open that old door again.

Maimie: I know what you mean, Leamy.

[Someone approaches from outside]

Maimie: Take the glasses, quick!

Mrs McCabe: Ah, wait for me, will you!

Dandy: C'mon. C'mon.

[LEAMY takes the glasses and hurries behind the counter. Enter DANDY MCCABE and his WIFE. His WIFE trails behind him, wearing a shawl]

Dandy: Good evening, Maimie!

Maimie: Dandy, Mrs McCabe.

Mrs McCabe: Hello, Maimie.

Maimie: What can I do for you?

Dandy: Give us a gargle first. *[To WIFE]* What do you want?

Mrs McCabe: A tint of peppermint.

Dandy: Give her a peppermint and give me a half o' rum.

Leamy: I'll get them, Muddy.

Maimie: Good boy, Leamy.

Dandy: Is the boss in?

Maimie: He should be back shortly.

Dandy: You'll do, just as nicely. I want to pay him for that acre of bog. Will you see if he has it in the books?

Maimie: Sit down, I won't be a minute.

[Exit MAIMIE]

Dandy: *[To WIFE]* C'mon, c'mon, c'mon, c'mon! Sit down there you, in a place where I can be admiring you.

[LEAMY emerges with drinks and places them on table]

Dandy: You're the oldest boy, aren't you?

Leamy: Yes sir!

Dandy: Call me Dandy, man. They all call it to me. Them that don't do it to my face, do it behind my back. What's your name?

Leamy:	Leamy!
Dandy:	Leamy, Dandy!
Leamy:	Leamy, Dandy!
Dandy:	You're called after your grandfather, Leamy Flanagan. A decent man he was. Too fond of his drop. A good man's case. How much is due to you?
Leamy:	Three shillings.
Dandy:	*[Locates money]* A horse and a hound is three shillings and a tanner for yourself.
Leamy:	Thanks very much.
Dandy:	Thanks very much, Dandy.
Leamy:	Thanks very much, Dandy.
Dandy:	Simple, isn't it? *[Indicates WIFE]* You know this one?
Leamy:	Yes, Dandy.
Dandy:	Married twenty-four years and never a cross word between us.
Leamy:	*[Beginning to enjoy himself]* That must be a record.
Dandy:	Say 'Dandy'.
Leamy:	That must be a record Dandy.
Dandy:	*[Conspiratorially]* And I'll tell you something else. To go no further. *[LEAMY nods]* If she liked she could be married to the Aly Khan.
	[The wife hits him on the arm and nearly collapses with laughter]
Dandy:	Met her when I was in the army. Love at first sight. Bet you can't guess why I brought her to town tonight . . . go on, guess.
Leamy:	I couldn't guess, Dandy.
Dandy:	*[Looks around mysteriously]* Word of a man. Shake hands on it. To go no further. *[LEAMY shakes his hand . . . conspiratorially . . .]* I'm buying an aeroplane for her.

[Wife hits him on arm and laughs to her heart's content. So does LEAMY]

Dandy: She has one weakness though, only the one . . .

Leamy: What's that, Dandy?

Dandy: She won't eat canaries. I boiled a canary for her yesterday and stuffed him with ginger. Wouldn't look at it . . . *[Laughter]* . . . had to give it to her mother.

[Enter MAIMIE with a ledger. LEAMY goes behind counter and puts money in cash register]

Maimie: *[Reading from ledger]* One acre of turbary purchased last January, including fees, thirty-six pounds ten. It's here all right, Dandy.

Dandy: And I'm here, too. *[Takes wallet from inside pocket and extracts money]* Here's your money, Maimie. Three tenners, a fiver, pound note, ten shillings, that's thirty-six pounds ten.

Maimie: *[Accepts money and counts it]* It's all here, Dandy.

Dandy: And I'm all there!

Maimie: I'll cross it off the book and get your receipt.

[MAIMIE goes behind counter to cash register and ledger. DANDY rises to his feet, finds MICK'S auctioneering hammer and fondles it briefly]

Dandy: Will I have another? *[To MRS McCABE]* Will you have one?

Mrs McCabe: Not for me.

Dandy: I'll have the same again, Leamy. *[Lifts hammer]* There's a hammer that never drove a nail. Ladies and gentlemen. I have here for sale, one prime farmer's wife, fifteen hands high, sound in wind and limb and steady as a butcher's table. Do I hear a bid . . . Do I hear a bid for this prime specimen of womanhood . . . *[To LEAMY]* You, sir! You look a decent sort of a man. Do I hear a bid . . . ? She has two medals for making toast and four for making pancakes. She have a gold cup for drinking sour milk and a certificate for snoring.

[Suddenly DANDY stops dead and looks towards the doorway. Enter the BULL McCABE, followed by TADHG, followed by the BIRD O'DONNELL. DANDY'S WIFE gets up immediately and stands near her husband]

Bull: You came, Dandy. Blood is thicker than water.

Dandy: *[Subdued, cautious]* How's the Bull? How are you, Tadhg . . . Bird?

[LEAMY quietly withdraws a little behind grocery counter. MAIMIE comes from behind counter]

Maimie: Your receipt, Dandy.

Dandy: Thanks, Maimie.

Bull: You got the word?

Dandy: Yes, Bull.

Bull: You know there's a man in the village who's here to wrong me?

Dandy: Yes, Bull! Yes!

Bull: Sit down! . . . All of you, sit down! Where's himself, Maimie?

[Enter MICK FLANAGAN]

Mick: Right behind you, Bull. Sorry I'm late.

Bull: *[Generously]* A good man is never late, Mick.

[All sit . . . MICK, the BIRD, TADHG, DANDY and his WIFE. MAIMIE goes forward and sits a little apart independently. BULL sees LEAMY behind the counter]

Bull: What's he doin' up? Shouldn't he be in bed?

Maimie: He's just going.

Bull: No . . . No . . . Let him up. He's no fool. He knows enough. Sit down, boy . . . *out here*, boy.

[LEAMY takes a seat near his mother]

Bull: I'm a fair man and I want nothing but what's mine! I won't be wronged in my own village, in my own country by an imported landgrabber. The sweat I've lost won't be given for nothing. A total stranger has come and he wants to bury my sweat and blood in concrete. It's ag'in' God an' man an' I was never the person to bow the head when trouble came and no man is goin' to do me out of my natural-born rights. Now this robber comes from nowhere and he's nothing less than a robber . . . And you all know the cure for a robber . . . he must be given a fright and a fright he's goin' to get. But people forgets old friends when there's danger and if this man gets a fright and a bit of a beatin', we'll have the civic guards goin' around askin' questions. Now, you know the kind civic guards is . . . What is friends for, I ask, unless 'tis to pull one another out of houlls. What is neighbours and relations for unless 'tis to 'love ye one another' says the Gospel. So, when the civic guards come with their long noses, all of you will remember that Tadhg and myself were in this pub at the time that robbin' gazebo got his dues . . . We'll give him just enough to teach him a lesson. Now, I'll want a promise, won't I, to show we can trust one another. Dandy, you'll take an oath on the Holy Ghost.

Dandy: Sure, Bull. Sure. And don't worry about the Missus.

Bull: Sound man, Dandy. I knew I could trust you. What about you, Bird?

Bird: OK, but I'm not swearing by the Holy Ghost.

Bull: And what have you got against the Holy Ghost, you little caffler, you?

Bird: 'Tis wrong! 'Tis wrong!

Bull: Did he ever give you a fright?

Bird: A fright?

Bull: Yes, a fright. Any other ghost you'll meet will frighten the life outa you. But the Holy Ghost never gave anyone a fright. Come on, swear!

Bird: Sure, Bull. Sure.

Bull: Mick?

Mick: OK, Bull, but don't overdo it.

Bull: A good fright and no more. Put up a bottle of whiskey for
                   my friends. Maimie . . . Maimie! I'm talkin' to you.

Maimie: And I hear you, Bull.

Bull: Maimie, what do you say?

Maimie: This man has done no harm.

Bull: Not yet . . . not yet . . . but he will.

Maimie: It isn't right to beat a man up. He's alone here.

Bull: He don't belong here.

Maimie: The guards will hear of it.

Bull: Of course they will, but that's the end of it as far as they
                   are concerned, if we all keep our mouths shut.

Maimie: This can lead to nothing but trouble.

Bull: There will be real trouble if you don't swear to keep your
                   trap shut. I know enough about you to cause a right plateful
                   of trouble. Your husband might be blind but the Bull
                   McCabe knows your comings and goings like the back of
                   his hand.

                   *[LEAMY looks curiously at his mother and then gets off stool
                   and tries to run past BULL. BULL stops him]*

Bull: And you, boy? You'll be all right, won't you? You don't
                   want your mother to be hurt, do you?

Maimie: Leamy won't say a word.

Bull: Of course he won't. There's men around here would think
                   nothing of puttin' a bomb up ag'in' a public house door.
                   'Twas done before, the time of the land division. Who's to
                   say what people will do?

                   [He pats LEAMY and dismisses him]

Maimie: All right! All right! We get the message.

Bull: That's great now. 'Tis a weight off my mind to know that
                   my friends are behind me. Now none of you will leave
                   here after me and Tadhg go and when we come back,
                   'twill be the same as if we never left. Right, Dandy?

Dandy: Sure thing, Bull.

Bull: Good health. Good health, Maimie.

Bird: Good luck, Bull.

Dandy: Good luck, Bull.

          [MICK rises and goes to the back of the bar]

Bull: What I would like now is a song and who better than
          Dandy.

Bird: Sure Bull.

Bull: Give us 'The Poor Blind Boy', Dandy.

          [DANDY commences to sing 'The Poor Blind Boy']

Dandy: *[Sings]*   She's left the old field where he played as a baby.
                    The little white cottage that lies by the sea.
                    The cradle that rocked him is lonesome and shady
                    As she thinks of those days that never will be.

          *[BULL motions to TADHG and they exit quietly. The singing
          goes on]*

                    They're far from each other, she cries for her
                       loved one
                    By night and by morning since ever he died,
                    She walked through the field while the cold moon
                       shines down
                    As she thinks of the fate of the poor blind boy.

          [End of Act One]

ACT TWO

Scene 1

[Action takes place at a gateway on the bóithrín near the main Carraigthomond Road. The time is midnight. Two figures are huddled together. They are the BULL McCABE and his son, TADHG. The BULL unwraps a small paper parcel and hands TADHG a sandwich.]

Bull: Eat that!

[TADHG accepts sandwich and takes a large bite from it. BULL carefully ties the parcel again and puts it in his pocket]

Tadhg: 'Tis bloody cold! *[Slapping between his armpits]*

Bull: 'Tis April, boy! 'Tis April. Listen and you can hear the first growth of the grass. The first music that was ever heard. That was a good bit o' sun today. A few more days like it and you won't know the face of the field.

Tadhg: D'you think he'll come?

Bull: Hard to say. Hard to say. You're sure you saw no sign of him all day.

Tadhg: Positive.

Bull: He wouldn't have come by the river unknown to you?

Tadhg: No chance! I hid in the shelter since we left the pub this morning and Johnny Sweeney was here till we came from the pub now. All I seen was crows . . . nothin' but crows. What do they be doing' . . . perched in the field all day? They weren't eatin' grass and they weren't diggin' snails. Just perched there, takin' no notice of anythin'. Do they be thinkin' like us?

Bull: I enjoy a crow as much as the next man. The first up in the morning is the crow and the soonest under his quilt.

Tadhg: I seen a few water-rats today.

Bull: Crafty sons o' whores!

Tadhg: They say that if the seed of man fails, the rats will take over the world.

Bull:	They're crafty, sure enough. But I could watch crows if there was time given for it. I often laughs at crows.
Tadhg:	Can they talk to one another? I'd swear they have a lingo all of their own.
Bull:	Who's to say? Who's to say? Anyway I have something else in my head besides the antics of crows.
Tadhg:	He'll never come now. 'Tis all hours of the night.
Bull:	We'll give it another half-hour and if he doesn't show up, we'll go to our beds. God knows I could sleep now, boy.
Tadhg:	And my Ma will be wondering.
Bull:	Let her wonder. You'll hear no complaint out of her.
Tadhg:	Da?
Bull:	What?
Tadhg:	Why don't yourself and Ma talk?
Bull:	Ah, hould your tongue!
Tadhg:	Ah, Da, come on! I always told you about my women.
Bull:	Your mother is a peculiar woman, son. I won't account for her. She's led me a queer life all these years.
Tadhg:	How long has it been?
Bull:	How long has what been?
Tadhg:	Since you spoke to her?
Bull:	Eat your sandwich, can't you. You have me addled.
Tadhg:	Ah tell us Da.
	[He sits near him]
Bull:	*[Rises, pauses and returns to* TADHG*]* Eighteen years since I slept with her or spoke to her.
Tadhg:	What was the cause?
Bull:	What was the cause but a tinker's pony . . . a hang-gallows piebald pony, a runty get of a gluttonous knacker with one eye. I was at the fair at Carraigthomond that day and she

gave permission to a tinker's widow to let the pony loose in one of the fields. The land was carryin' fourteen cows an' grass scarce. Fourteen cows, imagine! An' to go throwin' a pony in on top of them! Cripes, Tadhg, a tinker's pony would eat the hair off a child's head!

Tadhg: He would, Da, he would. But what happened between Ma and yourself?

Bull: God blast you! . . . that's what happened. Amn't I after tellin' you?

Tadhg: But after the pony, what happened?

Bull: I was in bed when she told me. I had a share of booze taken. I walloped her more than I meant, maybe. I went out and looked at the pony. He had one eye, a sightful right eye. I shot him through the two eyes, the blind and the good . . . a barrel at a time. It often played on my conscience. If 'twas as ass now, 'twouldn't matter, but a pony is a pony.

Tadhg: And she never spoke to you since?

Bull: Never a word. I tried to talk to her, to come round her. I put in electric light and bought the television. I built that godamned bathroom . . . *for her* . . . all over a tinker's nag, a dirty one-eyed pony. You'd swear he was human.

Tadhg: You had to do it, Da. Carrying fourteen cows. You had to do it.

Bull: Of course, I had to do it but she wouldn't see it that way. You understand all right, Tadhg. You're a sensible fellow who knows the ropes.

Tadhg: A tinker's pony would eat your finger-nails. Didn't you explain to her?

Bull: But you can't explain these things to women. It don't trouble them if the hay is scarce and the fields bald. I seen lonesome nights, Tadhg, lonesome nights. *[Comes suddenly upright]* Whisht! What was that?

[Sounds of a jet]

Tadhg: That's only a jet . . . one of them new ones with the high boomin' sound.

Bull: An aeroplane, is it?

Tadhg: That's all it is. I often hear them down here at night. I could tell you the different kinds.

Bull: *[Good-natured]* An' what do you be doin' down here at night? Eh? Not sayin' your prayers, I'll bet!

Tadhg: Oh, rambling around, watching out for donkeys.

[He slaps his armpits and moves around]

Bull: Women, I suppose! Anyone I know?

Tadhg: Ah, now, Da!

Bull: Ah, come on. Tell your oul' Da.

Tadhg: There's a daughter of Patsy Finnerty's.

Bull: I seen her. I seen her. A bit red in the legs but a good wedge of a woman. Can she milk?

Tadhg: As good as ourselves.

Bull: Can she handle pigs and feed cattle?

Tadhg: She knows more about them than myself.

Bull: If she does, she knows a lot.

Tadhg: She's a man by day but she's a woman at night.

Bull: And an only daughter into the bargain.

Tadhg: There's nine acres o' land.

Bull: I know there's nine. A good nine. Good man yourself. I reared you well. Did you question her?

Tadhg: I'd say she'd be willing enough. I wouldn't try to rush her, though. She's pampered and headstrong.

Bull: That will be knocked out of her.

Tadhg: Sometimes, I drops a hint and she doesn't seem unwilling to listen.

Bull: Nine acres o' land! Think of it! Keep your napper screwed on and we'll be important people yet, important people, boy!

Tadhg: Why do you think I'm chasing her?

Bull: What's that?

[He pulls TADHG back into the shadows at left. Two girl cyclists pass yahooing and giggling]

Girl 1: Come quickly, Bridie, I'll race you.

Girl 2: Ah, what's your hurry.

Tadhg: *[Crosses back into the light]* That's only a couple o' young ones on bicycles comin' home from the picture in Carraigthomond. Calm yourself, Da. You're very jittery.

Bull: 'Tis cold. I'm used to the bed at this hour.

Tadhg: If he's to come, he'll come.

Bull: If he doesn't come in ten minutes I'm givin' it over. All we'll get here is pneumonia . . . Whisht! . . . that's surely somebody now . . .

[They both listen]

Tadhg: You're right and, whoever it is, he's in a hurry . . . Stay cool now! Stay cool!

[They both withdraw into darkness as steps grow louder. TADHG takes a cap from his pocket and quickly draws it fully over his head. As the approaching party draws nearer, whistling can be heard. Enter the BIRD, out of breath and whistling. He looks around and walks from one end of the stage to the other, calling]

Bird: Bull? . . . Tadhg? . . . Any of you there? Bull, 'tis me, the Bird . . . Tadhg?

[There is no answer and the BIRD is uncomfortable]

Bird: Ah, lads, if you're there, don't be codding me. Come on out. I'm after runnin' from Carraigthomond with a bad heart . . .

[He turns away despondently. At this the BULL and TADHG leap out from their hiding places, shouting and leaping, so that the BIRD rushes from one to another terror-stricken and is forced to sit down. BULL and TADHG laugh uproariously]

Bird: Ye nearly put me off in a weakness. My heart is flutterin' like the engine of a motor-bike.

Bull: That's a terrible pity, Tadhg, isn't it? Bird, if I thought you were a drinkin' man I'd run myself to Carraigthomond to get a glass of brandy for you.

Bird: All right, then . . . be funny . . . and I'll keep my mouth shut . . . about what I know.

[BULL suddenly seizes BIRD by the throat and lifts him to his feet]

Bull: What do you know, ferret? Spit it out or 'twill be spat for you! *[Releasing him]* Come on! Out with it!

Bird: He was in Flanagan's for a drink. I was at the counter talking to Maimie. He said he was going to his lodgings for his coat to have a look at the field.

Bull: So he won't heed my warning.

Bird: Oh, this is the field he fancies all right. It's like love at first sight. Like fallin' for a woman.

Bull: *[Impatiently]* Did you see him?

Bird: He was on the road behind me. That's why I ran. Don't forget who tipped you off, Bull.

Bull: Be sure we won't.

[The BIRD disappears into the darkness]

Tadhg: Listen. *[He listens]* It's bound to be him.

Bull: Who else could it be! . . . Pull back . . .He's comin' near.

[BULL and TADHG withdraw into the shadows. Enter WILLIAM. He wears a light raincoat.
   Hearing a sound, he stiffens and looks about him suspiciously. BULL emerges from the shadows]

Bull: Turn around and go home!

William: Who the hell do you think you are? I have as much right to be here as you.

Bull:	I'm telling you now for the last time . . . turn around and go home!
	[WILLIAM pauses, undecided. BULL flexes the ashplant in his hand]
William:	I'm legally entitled to look at this field.
Bull:	I want your solemn oath that you'll leave Carraigthomond first thing in the morning and never set foot here again. Your solemn oath!
William:	Don't you threaten me!
Bull:	You'll do as your told or your wife won't know you when she sees you again . . . an' I'm not foolin' you, boy!
William:	For God's sake, get out of my way.
	[He endeavours to advance but the BULL draws a sweeping blow with his ashplant which WILLIAM narrowly avoids]
William:	Hey, that's dangerous!
Bull:	Your solemn oath! Come on, your solemn oath that you'll quit Carraigthomond and never come back.
William:	Come on, have a bit of sense.
	[He tries to advance again but the BULL repels him with the stick. Then the BULL drops the stick]
Bull:	Come on! Pass us, if you're able!
	[Behind him, silently, TADHG emerges from the darkness]
Bull:	*[To WILLIAM]* Come on, if you fancy yourself.
William:	You won't goad me into assaulting you. A good night's sleep and you might see things a little clearer.
	[WILLIAM attempts to pass BULL but TADHG jumps on him from behind, hits him on back of head and knocks him to ground]
Bull:	Hold on to him!
	[TADHG holds WILLIAM's arms and BULL hits him heavily, skilfully, three or four times. WILLIAM breaks from them,

weakly desperate, but TADHG *grabs him by the legs and brings him to the ground again.* BULL *grabs his stick and beats* WILLIAM *across the back and head.* WILLIAM'S *screaming dies out.* TADHG *pulls* WILLIAM *up as the* BULL *stops beating him with his stick and gives* WILLIAM *the knee.* WILLIAM *falls helplessly.* BIRD *rushes to* TADHG]

Bird: In the name of God, stop! . . . stop! . . . or you'll do for him.

*[*TADHG *throws* BIRD *aside and gets in a crucial kick at* WILLIAM'S *head]*

Bull: Stop it! . . . Stop it! That's enough. We only want to frighten him.

Tadhg: That's what he wanted, wasn't it?

Bull: *[Pulling him away]* Now, if there's any questions about this, where were we tonight? What were we doing? . . . We were in the pub, the three of us. 'Tis ag'in the law but 'tis a sound excuse. Agreed? All to be on the one word. Come on now across the fields. That way we won't be seen . . . Move!

Bird: You're after going too far. I don't like the look of him.

Bull: Get back to the pub!

[The BULL *pushes them off and turns to look down at* WILLIAM]

Bull: Why couldn't you stay away, you foolish boy? Look at the trouble you drew on yourself, you headstrong foolish boy, with your wife and family depending on you . . . Jesus Christ —

[He kneels and examines WILLIAM. *He is suddenly aware that* WILLIAM *is dead. He looks desperately around, then rises and remains looking down at* WILLIAM. *He then suddenly kneels and takes* WILLIAM'S *head in his lap and whispers an act of contrition. Looks around him and disappears into the night]*

Scene 2

[LEAMY and MAIMIE preparing to leave for Mass]

Maimie:	*[Ad lib]* Put their scarves and hats on, Aoife.
Aoife:	*[Ad lib]* Give me your hand. Off you go, wait for me at the corner.
Leamy:	Has the bishop spoken here before?
Maimie:	I can't remember. Your father would know.
Leamy:	Muddy . . . . ?
Maimie:	Yes, love?
Leamy:	Muddy, why are the Bull McCabe and Tadhg and my father and the Sergeant such bullies?
Maimie:	The McCabes are bullies. Your father isn't a real bully and the Sergeant isn't a real bully.
Leamy:	Oh, but they are!
Maimie:	Aoife, take the girls to Mass.
Leamy:	Do you remember the day of the big hurling match, when the Blezzop brothers nearly beat the man to death . . .
Maimie:	Yes.
Leamy:	Well, afterwards, they came into the pub and my father served them with drinks. He started praising them and telling them they were great men and then the small man, Mr Broderick, said to the older brother, 'Out of my way, I wouldn't drink in the same house with the likes of you', and then the Blezzop brothers attacked him and were beating him up. I wanted to run out from behind the counter and help Mr Broderick, but what could I do? So I ran up to the barracks and told the guard on duty. It was two hours later the Sergeant came down.
Maimie:	Leamy!
Leamy:	He asked my father if everything was all right and my father said it was. I was so ashamed. Later on, the guard who was on duty came in and himself and my father were saying that Mr Broderick was an awkward man and that he'd look out for him in the future . . .

Maimie: It's time to go to Mass, love!

Leamy: I was thinking of goin' to the barracks again and telling
                  the Sergeant about the Bull.

Maimie: No . . . not this time! There are hundred of guards, and
                  detectives and the pressure is on for the first time and it's
                  on from the outside. The Bull McCabe won't suffer, Leamy.
                  A few years in jail or a dismissal, but it's you, Leamy . . .
                  it's you who will suffer because, don't you see, it's you
                  who will have done all the work and you'll be a freak for
                  ever more, different from the rest of us.

Leamy: But I want to be different from them, Muddy!

Maimie: Do you love me, Leamy?

Leamy: Yes.

Maimie: Then say no more about this. If you love me and trust me,
                  you will say no more . . . never again until my family is
                  reared and able to look out for themselves.

Leamy: Are you afraid, Mud?

Maimie: I was never afraid once. I feared nothing that walked
                  the face of the earth until my first child was born. A child
                  makes a prisoner of a woman, but Leamy, you're a lovely
                  gaoler . . . come on to Mass . . .

                  [They start to cross to exit]

Maimie: God, we're a pity, Leamy . . . the whole bunch of us.

Leamy: Except for the small man, that Mr Broderick, and he's
                  gone to England. He was no pity. He was a brave man.

Maimie: Promise me, on your word of honour, no more talk about
                  the killing. No matter who asks you.

Leamy: Yes, Muddy. I promise. I'll always do whatever you tell me.

Maimie: *[Heartbroken]* And what can I tell you, love?

                  *[LEAMY exits. MAIMIE follows into church. They take their
                  place among the parishoners and we cut to the bishop's
                  sermon]*

Bishop: 'Do not be afraid of those who kill the body but cannot kill the soul. But rather be afraid of him who is able to destroy both body and soul in Hell.'

In the name of the Father and of the Son and of the Holy Ghost, Amen.

Dearly beloved brethren, these are the words of Christ Himself. He was speaking about truth. How many of you would deny Christ? How many of you, like Peter, would stand up and say: 'I know not the Man!' but you can lie without saying a word; you can lie without opening your lips; you can lie by silence.

Five weeks ago in this parish, a man was murdered — he was brutally beaten to death. For five weeks the police have investigated and not one single person has come forward to assist them. Everywhere they turned, they were met by silence, a silence of the most frightful and diabolical kind — the silence of the lie. In God's name, I beg you, I implore you, if any of you knows anything, to come forward and to speak without fear.

This is a parish in which you understand hunger. But there are many hungers. There is a hunger for food — a natural hunger. There is the hunger of the flesh — a natural understandable hunger. There is a hunger for home, for love, for children. These things are good — they are good because they are necessary. But there is also the hunger for land. And in this parish, you, and your fathers before you knew what it was to starve because you did not own your own land — and that has increased; this unappeasable hunger for land. But how far are you prepared to go to satisfy this hunger. Are you prepared to go to the point of robbery? Are you prepared to go to the point of murder? Are you prepared to kill for land? Was this man killed for land? Did he give his life's blood for a field? If so, that field will be a field of blood and it will be paid for in thirty pieces of silver — the price of Christ's betrayal — and you, by your silence will share in that betrayal.

Among you there is a murderer! You may even know his name, you may even have seen him commit this terrible crime — through your silence, you share his guilt, your innocent children will grow up under the shadow of this

terrible crime, and you will carry this guilt with you until
you face your Maker at the moment of judgement . . .

If you are afraid to go to the police, then come to your
priests, or come to me. And if there is one man among
you — one man made after Christ's likeness — he will stand
up and say: 'There! There he is! There is the murderer!'
And that man will have acknowledged Christ before men
and Christ will acknowledge him before His Father in
Heaven. But if you, by your silence, deny Christ before men,
He will disown you in Heaven, and I, as His representative,
will have a solemn duty to perform. I will place this parish
under interdict and then there will be a silence more
terrible than the first. The church bell will be silent: the
mass bell will not be heard; the voice of the confessional
will be stilled and in your last moment will be the most
dreadful silence of all for you will go to face your Maker
without the last sacrament on your lips . . . and all because
of your silence now. In God's name, I beg of you to speak
before it is too late. 'I am the way, says Christ, and the truth.
Do not be afraid of those who can kill the body but cannot
kill the soul. But rather, be afraid of him who can destroy
both body and soul in hell'.

In the name of the Father and of the Son and of the
Holy Ghost, Amen.

Scene 3

[Action takes place in the bar of MICK FLANAGAN's public house.
The time is evening, five days later.

Present are MICK FLANAGAN, the BULL McCABE, his son, TADHG, the BIRD O'
DONNELL MAGGIE BUTLER and DANDY McCABE.

MICK FLANAGAN stands behind the counter.

The BULL McCABE is in process of counting money which is being
accepted by MICK]

Bull: *[Counting at table]* £310 . . . £320 . . . £330 . . . £340 . . .
£350 *[To MAGGIE]* Now, no one can say you didn't get a
fair price. *[To MICK]* I'll have a receipt for that.

Mick: I have it here for you.

*[MICK locates a receipt book and commences to write. The
BULL accepts. MICK takes the money and goes to MAGGIE. He
puts money in MAGGIE's lap, while all stand around]*

Mick: Here's your money. 'Tis all there, every penny of £350. It's a fine bundle of notes.

Bull: Honest got and honest given . . . and now, Mick Flanagan, fill a drink for the house.

[MICK goes behind bar]

Bird: A drop of whiskey for me.

Dandy: A jigger o' rum.

Bull: Give 'em whatever they want. 'Tisn't everyday that this class o' money makes an appearance.

Bird: 'Tis a high pile o' money. You're blessed with luck in the decent man you met, Mrs Butler.

Maggie: I have the money taken now and there's no more to be said.

Tadhg: 'Tis a fair exchange, considering.

Maggie: So you say, but there's many that think that £800 would have been fairer.

Bull: All gossip . . . nothing but jealous gossip by nosey neighbours who couldn't pay for the site of a sitdown lavatory, not to mind a field. They're great warrants to talk but when it comes to forkin' out the cash, where are they? I am the man with the money — hard-earned and got fair — and I'm not ashamed to say, 'twas the last penny I possessed.

Tadhg: 'Twas every half-penny we owned and we had to flog five heifers to put it together.

Bull: God, I was lonesome after that little yellow heifer.

Tadhg: She was a beauty.

Bull: She was a little queen, boy! The step of this one was like a dropping leaf, Dandy.

Tadhg: The other four were real ladies too. They were shapely cattle, by God they were. They sold well, Da. You'll have to admit that.

Bull: And we had to borrow from the bank. We're paupers but isn't it better to be a pauper and have a clean conscience about your debts?

Bird: Oh, by God, that's well spoken.

Dandy: Nicely thrown together. Nicely.

Bull: Isn't it better to have our principles than be millionaires. Isn't it, Tadhg?

Tadhg: You're a straight man, Da.

Dandy: None straighter.

Bull: If a man isn't straight, he might as well be dead.

Bird: I admire a straight man.

               [MICK serves them with drinks]

Bull: I grudge no man his property, but a lot of the hangin' thieves begrudge me.

Tadhg: 'Tis all jealousy.

Bull: *[Paying for drinks]* Jealousy and spite . . . here's the good health to all of us . . .

All: Good luck.

Bull: We have as fine a farm now as the best and maybe more to come and a woman with it, eh Tadhg?

Tadhg: 'Twon't be my fault!

Bull: In the course of time, as the man said: in the course of time.

Bird: And a fine heifer she is, too!

Bull: Good legs and a great bussom, God bless the girl!

Bird: Oh, God bless her again.

Dandy: *[Finishing his drink]* Long life to her!

Bull: She's a good milker.

Dandy: For a fact!

Tadhg: A mighty milker!

Bull: With nine acres!

Dandy: Nine!

Bird:	Knows her banbh and her pig. Strong, too, and not bad-lookin' when you get used to her.
Bull:	She's all that, God bless her.
Mick:	Father Murphy . . . !
	[Enter SERGEANT LEAHY followed by the priest, FATHER MURPHY]
Bull:	*[Seemingly unaware of the new arrivals . . . to MAGGIE]* Mrs Butler, from this out, we'll give you a lift to Mass every Sunday. 'Tis too long a walk for an old woman.
Bird:	*[Tips BULL'S chest]* There's a big heart in there: an outsize heart that's too big for this world but God don't miss nothin' an' 'tis wrote down in Heaven in red letters like blood.
Dandy:	Well spoke, Bird! Well spoke! Is the names of his friends there?
Bird:	*[Sanctimonious, mocking]* Wrote down there, my child, is the names of all the faithful.
Bull:	That's a kindly thing to say, Bird. Ah, Father Murphy, if 'tisn't against rules of the Church, could I get a little drop of something for you, Father? Or are the clergy not allowed to take sup in the pubs?
Fr Murphy:	No, thank you, Mr McCabe but I will take a bottle of orange if the Sergeant here joins me.
	[BIRD nudges TADHG]
Sergeant:	I'll have an orange.
Bull:	And welcome you are to whatever you like.
	[MAIMIE enters]
Maimie:	Good morning, Father.
Fr Murphy:	Good morning, Mrs Flanagan.
	[MICK gives MAIMIE the beck and she goes to left of bar, out of the way]
Bird:	Not a bad day outside, Father.

Fr Murphy: Nice and fresh but a bit chilly.

Bull: There's a good share of sun now, considering.

Tadhg: There's good growth.

Bird: There's amazing growth for the time of year.

Dandy: I seen buds on every bush on the way in.

Bird: Buds, imagine, so early!

Tadhg: Make a good summer!

Bull: The meadows will be early; early buds, early meadows. How're you for hay, Dandy?

Dandy: I'll pull through, Bull. I've a share of turnips yet.

Fr Murphy: Better come to the point. This morning, Sergeant Leahy and I are making house to house calls. Our job is not a pleasant one but alas, 'tis a necessary one.

Bull: It sounds like a collection.

Sergeant: It's a collection all right, but this time we're collecting information.

Fr Murphy: And I hope you'll be more liberal with it than you are with your money.

    [There is an awkward silence which MICK breaks by placing drinks for the newcomers on the counter. BULL pays]

Fr Murphy: There's nothing to fear. Anything you tell us will be held in the strictest confidence. This is a job which nobody likes but someone must do it or a murderer will be allowed to go free . . . I hope you have no objections, Mick, at our barging in like this.

Mick: Oh, good God, no, Father! Not at all! Anything I can do, I'll do.

Bull: Whatever is in our power to be done, will be done, right, Bird? Right, Tadhg? Whatever is in our power by the grace of God.

Sergeant: Then we'll begin with you, Mrs Butler. And if the rest of you wouldn't mind waiting in the back room for a moment or two, we'll begin right away.

[All look at BULL]

Bull: It can never be said that we stood in the way of the law. Come on, Tadhg! Come on, Bird . . . Dandy!

Mick: This way, gentlemen, you know where to go.

[The four exit]

Fr Murphy: Now, Mrs Butler. This is neither official nor formal. All we want is a little chat and whatever you have to tell us, will go no further.

Maggie: Yes, Father.

Fr Murphy: You heard the Bishop's appeal on Sunday last?

Maggie: Yes, Father.

Fr Murphy: Unfortunately, it seems to have fallen on deaf ears. Now the Sergeant here assures me that the slightest bit of information might easily break the case. Now, Mrs Butler, you live near where the body was found . . . where the murder actually took place. Did you see or hear anything on the night?

[MAGGIE entwines her fingers but does not reply and the priest exchanges looks with the sergeant]

Sergeant: Anything at all, Mrs Butler?

Fr Murphy: Did you hear or see anything? It doesn't matter what. Even a little thing might help the Sergeant.

Maggie: 'Tis me needs the help, God help me.

Sergeant: You met the man didn't you? On the morning of the day he was killed.

Maggie: He was in here all right, that morning. He was a nice man . . . a bit strong-willed.

Fr Murphy: Most men are!

Sergeant: Did anything take place on that day? Was anything said?

Maggie: If there was, I have it forgotten by now. I have no memory at all. 'Twas often a Saturday when I drew my pension, even though I'd want the money.

Sergeant: Had the dead man an argument with the Bull McCabe?

Maggie: If he did, I don't remember it. I hate fighting or noise.

Fr Murphy: Mrs Butler, if you know anything, don't be afraid to tell us. Nothing will happen to you.

Maggie: I'm a lone widow, living on the side of the road with no one to look after me.

Fr Murphy: We understand perfectly, Mrs Butler, but place yourself in God's hands and you need have no fear. If you're afraid of anyone, the Sergeant will caution that person and you can be assured of peace and privacy.

Sergeant: I'll go to the person and tell him that if he so much looks at you sideways, it will be as much as his life is worth.

Maggie: Oh, no . . . no . . . you mustn't . . . you mustn't . . . You can't.

Sergeant: So there is a person . . . someone you fear. *[Gently]* Who is it, Mrs Butler? It is your duty to tell us.

Maggie: I'm an old woman, living alone, and I do be worryin' nights. I have no one with me.

Sergeant: We all have to worry nights, no matter who we are.

Maggie: I don't live in the barracks with guards in all the rooms. An old woman . . . a woman drawing her pension that wants to be left alone . . . I never did harm to no one . . . I only ask to be left alone.

[She becomes silent. SERGEANT and PRIEST exchange looks]

Fr Murphy: *[Kindly]* Very well, Mrs Butler. You can go now.

[MAGGIES rises and goes to exit]

Maggie: God bless you, Father . . . and pray for me. Pray for me, Father!

Fr Murphy: God bless you, Mrs Butler. I will pray for you.

Sergeant: Good day to you, Mrs Butler.

[Exit MAGGIE]

Fr Murphy:	*[To SERGEANT]* Sorry, Tom! I was certain that, after the sermon and with the informal approach, you might learn something.
Sergeant:	It's not your fault, Father. You can't beat fear and ignorance. You're up against a stone wall.
Fr Murphy:	What about Mick Flanagan? Do you want to question him?
Sergeant:	Waste of time! Too crafty! He's been questioned ten times already.
Fr Murphy:	What about Dandy?
Sergeant:	Dandy and the Bull are first cousins. There's no hope there. Dandy would be all right if it weren't for Tadhg and the Bull.
Fr Murphy:	The young lad, Leamy?
Sergeant:	The mother has him sworn to silence. He'll never renege on her. His lips are stitched forever.
Fr Murphy:	He won't easily bear the burden of that legacy in the years ahead of him. *[Pause]* What about Mrs Flanagan herself then? She wasn't questioned before.
Sergeant:	Maimie! It might be worth a try, at that.
Fr Murphy:	You're a good-looking fellow, Tom. That might hold.
Sergeant:	*[Laughs, turns and puts down drink]* With all due respects to you, Father, I'd chance anything if I thought 'twould solve the crime.
Fr Murphy:	You needn't go that far! Anyway, two wrongs don't make a right.
Sergeant:	You wouldn't say that if you had my job.
	[He calls MICK from back room. Enter MICK]
Fr Murphy:	If you've no objection, we'd like to talk to your wife.
Mick:	I've no objection, if she hasn't. I'll call her. *[Goes to the stairway; calls]* Maimie, you're wanted.
Maimie:	*[Offstage; Calls back]* I'll be down in a minute.
Mick:	You won't get much out of Maimie, if she's in a sulk.
Sergeant:	Strange, isn't it, Mick, the way nobody knows anything about anything?

Mick: Ah, 'tis a terrible state of affairs! Of course it's not our job.
                 My job is auctioneering. Father Murphy says mass and it's
                 up to the guards to catch the murderer.

Sergeant: If the public won't co-operate, there's nothing the guards
                 can do.

Mick: They'll get their wages, no matter what happens.

Fr Murphy: But the public, Mick. They've . . .

Mick: Ah, come off it now, Father! The public aren't getting paid.
                 'Tis the other way around. We're payin' the guards and
                 when they can't do their job they blame it on the public.
                 No reflections on you, Sergeant. God knows, you're a
                 sound man at your job.

                 [Enter MAIMIE]

Maimie: All right! I confess everything! I killed him! I've said
                 goodbye to the kids. *[Raises her hands over her head]*
                 Take me, Sergeant.

Fr Murphy: This isn't a laughing matter, Mrs Flanagan. A man has
                 been murdered, a murder isn't a joke.

Maimie: All right! So a man has been murdered! What's it to me?
                 I've nine kids to look after. Look at the state of me from
                 cooking and scrubbing and scraping but, thank God, I'm
                 off on my annual holidays soon.

Sergeant: What annual holidays?

Maimie: I'm pregnant again, so I'll have a holiday with the new
                 baby; the only one we'll ever have together.

Mick: Ah, now, Maimie, not in front of Fr Murphy.

Maimie: You're the fault of it, goddam you! Just look at him. You'd
                 think butter wouldn't melt in his mouth.

Mick: Ah, Maimie . . .

Maimie: I'll be carrying all through the summer. All over you! . . .
                 My head is gone queer from it! . . . what was it you
                 wanted me for, Father?

Fr Murphy: It's in connection with the murder.

Maimie: He did it . . . take him away! I'd swear him to the gallows if I thought I could spend a year without having a baby.

Sergeant: Seriously, Maimie.

Maimie: I'm serious, Sergeant. I'm more serious than you.

Sergeant: I think maybe you can help us. You may be the one who can break this case.

Maimie: Me! How can I help you?

Sergeant: Well, you met the dead man. He was here the day of the auction. Did you hear or see anything that might help us?

Maimie: Hear or see anything! What in the name of God are you talking about?

Sergeant: The Bull McCabe was here that day?

Maimie: He was.

Sergeant: Didn't he have an argument with the dead man?

Maimie: You can't argue with a dead man!

Sergeant: Don't mock this dead man. He was murdered!

Maimie: And don't talk to me, you yahoo from God-knows-where!

Fr Murphy: You're sure nothing was said?

Maimie: I don't remember it. They seemed quite friendly to me.

Sergeant: Quite friendly?

Maimie: No, not quite friendly! I should have said fairly friendly or a kind of friendly. What kind of friendly would you like? Would reasonably friendly do, or would it convict me?

Sergeant: *[Anger]* For God's sake, Maimie . . . was anything said?

Maimie: Yes . . . but don't ask me what was said. A woman has a head like a sieve and a woman expecting for the tenth time should have her head examined! How well they wouldn't murder me! No such luck! I'll have to stay alive and look at thicks like you climbing on other people's backs because you have authority.

Fr Murphy: You have nothing to tell us?

Maimie:	What do you think I am? A bloody schoolgirl, is it?
Sergeant:	You were here the night of the murder?
Maimie:	I'm always here! Always! Now, for Christ's sake, get out of here and let me alone till I get the dinner.
	[Exit MAIMIE]
Mick:	She's in the sulks today. 'Tis me will pay for it now for the next seven or eight months. A pregnant woman is worse than a bloody volcano.
Sergeant:	You told the investigators that the Bull and his son were here the night of the murder.
Mick:	And so they were!
Sergeant:	You're sure of that?
Mick:	God Almighty, didn't I tell it to four different detectives with notebooks. All taken down different like the Four Gospels, but all on the one word when the man is crucified, whoever he is.
Sergeant:	And the Bird, was he here too?
Mick:	You know damn well, he was! What's the point in repeating these questions?
Fr Murphy:	Now, Mick, the Sergeant has his job to do. There's nothing personal.
Mick:	Yes, but goddamit I've told him the same thing a hundred times and he still tries to make me out a liar. He'll go too far. He wouldn't be the first Sergeant to be transferred. I always voted right.
Sergeant:	I'm well aware of how you vote. Will you tell the Bird I want him.
Mick:	Very well. But hurry it up. What will the neighbours think, the Sergeant and the priest here all morning? 'Tis how they'll think I'm the murderer.
Sergeant:	Don't worry, Mick. Everybody knows that it wasn't you, because everybody knows that it was another man . . . maybe two men.

Mick: 'Tis your job to find out.

         [Exit MICK]

Sergeant: I won't be transferred . . . 'twould be too much to expect.

         [Enter the BIRD]

Bird: More questions?

Sergeant: You don't have to answer.

Bird: I'll answer. I'll co-operate. That's one thing about the Bird —
         co-operation. None of us can get along without it. If there
         was more co-operation the world would be an easier place.
         Am I right, Father?

Fr Murphy: The Sergeant wants to talk to you.

Bird: You can depend on the Bird. Now, Sergeant, what can I do
         for you?

Sergeant: The night of the murder . . .

Bird: Yes, of course . . .

Sergeant: You say you were here at the time with the Bull McCabe
         and his son . . . in their company.

Bird: That is correct. Exactly what was spoken. Dead right there
         for a start, anyway, and a big change from the plain-clothes.

Sergeant: As far as I remember, Bird, the Bull was never a friend of
         yours. How come, then, that you spent a night drinking
         together?

Bird: I'll forgive any man, Sergeant . . . any man. Let bygones
         be bygones is my policy.

Sergeant: You're sure you weren't anywhere near Maggie Butler's
         field over the river that night?

Bird: Neither near it nor within it. Arrived here at Flanagan's pub,
         time . . . 9.25 pm. Joined forces with my two friends.
         Did remain with associates on the premises till 2.45 am.
         Arrived home at 3 am sharp. Fried sausages one pound
         and one half and one ring of pudding white. Made pot of
         tea for self, Bull McCabe and son, Tadhg. Did say goodnight

to same who departed for home. Was in bed at 3.45 pm and that's my story, long enough, as told to seven different detectives on seven different occasions and as told to yourself and His Reverence right now on this day of our Lord, 1965, Amen.

Sergeant: And very nicely put together, too! Do you have any ideas about who might have killed this man?

Bird: I am of the opinion the crime was committed by tinkers or if 'twasn't tinkers 'twas done by persons unknown. They are the biggest blackguards of all, those persons unknown. You see they does everything unknown to people so no one knows who they are. Definitely, persons unknown.

Sergeant: I see . . . and have you any proof of this?

Bird: It's only my opinion, Sergeant . . . and it was only my opinion that you wanted. Opinions is not evidence, Father!

Sergeant: I'll watch you night and day from this on, you dirty, little sewer-rat. I'll haunt you, because I know as well as you do who committed the murder . . . And I think you were present when it happened.

Bird: If I was a big noise you wouldn't haunt me, Sergeant. You know who to haunt, all right!

Sergeant: It is my opinion, Bird, that you witnessed this murder and that your silence was bought for a few pounds. How much did you get? £5 . . . £10 . . . £20? Look, Bird, I'll guarantee you £500, £500 in hard cash, if you'll give me a hint. No one will know where the information came from.

Bird: If I took that £500, you'd be trying to solve a second murder, and you'd be no nearer than you are to solving this one.

Fr Murphy: Who are you afraid of, Bird?

Sergeant: The Bull, is it? Or Tadhg?

Fr Murphy: Or both?

Sergeant: £500.

Bird: 'Twould just about pay the expenses of my funeral.

Sergeant: It wouldn't be your funeral!

Bird:	Are you guaranteeing that as well? I have to live, and what's more, I have to live in Carraigthomond, murder or no bloody murder.
	[BIRD turns to exit]
Fr Murphy:	Bird!
	[BIRD stops]
Sergeant:	Let him go!
	[BIRD exits]
Sergeant:	McCabe and his son killed this man. You know, I know and the whole village knows. Nobody cares and the terrible thing is that nobody ever will care.
	[Enter the BULL, TADHG and DANDY]
Bull:	How long more are you going to keep us stuck back here like prisoners of war?
Fr Murphy:	We're sorry, Mr McCabe. The rotation was accidental.
Bull:	Ah, that's all right, Father. We understand.
Sergeant:	Bull . . . Bull . . . Will you answer me one question?
Bull:	If I'm able.
Sergeant:	Which of you killed him?
Bull:	Well, now, I'm damn downright glad you asked me that because I have a fair idea. *[Becomes confidential]* The wits was often frightened out of me, too, many a night, not knowing the minute a band of tinkers would break out from a bush and hammer my brains out. Try the camp of the Gorleys and if it isn't one of the Gorleys, try the McLaffertys, and if it 'tisn't one of them, 'tis sure to be one of the Mulligans. Don't they kill one another, not to mind killing a Christian?
Tadhg:	God, yes, Da! Yes! They're a terror!
Bull:	Or whose to say 'twasn't an ass or a stallion. I heard of an ass kicking an oul' woman to death up the country some-where. My wife was run out of the haggard by two Spanish

	mares of a day — two crotchety bitches who'd as soon eat you as kick you. And ask Dandy there, Dandy's wife was chased by a piebald ass, a stallion. Isn't that right, Dandy?
Dandy:	She lost her voice for a week from the fright she got. And she woke with nightmares nine nights running.
Sergeant:	Very touching! Thanks for the help, Dandy, You can go now.
Bull:	Good man, Dandy, mind yourself. And do you know another thing . . . and this might be the answer. Ask the ordinary man and that's where's the answer.
Sergeant:	Yes?
Bull:	What took him down there at that time of the night? What would take you down there, Tadhg?
Tadhg:	A woman is the only thing that would carry me.
Bull:	And a woman it was, believe me! Isn't all the murders over women? 'Twas surely a woman.
Sergeant:	You think so?
Bull:	Some doxy with no grazing of her own. What brought him without his wife, eh? Another woman was the draw . . . maybe a married woman, in pardon to you, Father. There they were, hobnobbing and cronawning under a bush when the woman's husband arrived. Can you blame the poor man, Father? In all fairity can you blame him for murderin' a home-wrecker. Don't be too hard on him, Sergeant, when you catch him.
Sergeant:	It wasn't tinkers, Bull. It wasn't a donkey and it wasn't a jealous husband. Now, was it?
Bull:	*[Passionately]* And, by God, it wasn't Bull McCabe and it wasn't Tadhg and Tadhg and me are sick of your dirty, informer's tactics. You've been after us now, since the donkey was kilt. We're watching your shifty peeler's questions. The two of you there have the power behind you. Why isn't it some other man you picked, Sergeant, to go searching with you? Like the labourer or the servant boy? Why isn't it a ploughman or the Council worker? No . . . you picked one of the gang. If 'twasn't the priest,

'twould be the doctor or the school-master or the shop-keeper. You have the law well sewn up, all of you . . . all nice and tidy to yourselves.

Fr Murphy: *[Hurt]* That's not true! You're deliberately twisting . . .

Bull: Christ had no guard's uniform and He had no white collar around His neck. But He picked a gang of small farmers and poachers. They had their cross like all poor people, and that held them together. If a poor man does something wrong he gets a guard's baton on the poll and he's lugged up the barracks. But, if 'tis the doctor or the schoolmaster or the lawman, they say, 'tis tough on them but there's a way out and the law is law no more.

Sergeant: See here now . . .

Fr Murphy: Let him go on!

Bull: I seen an ould priest last year, as called to our house outside. He sat down near me and spoke to Tadhg and me about hard luck, about dead-born calves and the cripples you meet among dropped calves. He ate with us and he got sick after it . . . fat mate but he ate it and by God, he had a shine of us and said he wished he was like us. I gave him a pound and Tadhg gave him seven and a tanner and if he wanted to stay with us for a year, we'd have kept him. But I won't pay you no Christmas dues, Father . . . not no more . . . and there's no law against that . . . Were we fond of him, Tadhg, of that ould priest?

Tadhg: We were, Da, we were. He was one of our own.

Mick: I'll have to ask you to go now, Father. What will the village think if ye don't leave? We have a family to think of.

Sergeant: You're a cleverer man than I took you for, Bull!

Bull: The likes of us that's ignorant has to be clever.

Sergeant: Did you see the dead man's widow at the funeral, Bull?

Bull: I saw her . . . wasn't Tadhg and myself the first to sympathise?

Fr Murphy: We can't beat the public, Tom.

Sergeant: It's what the public wants.

Fr Murphy: But they never really get what they want.

Bull: Don't we now. You're wrong there, Father. You have
                   your collar and the Sergeant, his uniform. I have my fields
                   and Tadhg, *[To TADHG]* remember this. There's two laws.
                   There's a law for them that's priests and doctors and
                   lawmen. But there's no law for us. The man with the
                   law behind him is the law . . . and it don't change and
                   it never will.

Fr Murphy: Do you ever think of God . . . any of you?

Bull: He's the man I says my prayers to, and I argues with Him
                   sometimes.

Fr Murphy: About what?

Bull: Same as you, 'cos I'm the same kind of creature as you.

Fr Murphy: The Sergeant asked you if you spoke with the widow and
                   you said you did. Did you feel pity for her?

Bull: I'm like you. I can't support her 'cos I'm married myself
                   and you'll hardly throw off the collar and marry her . . .
                   When you'll be gone, Father, to be a Canon somewhere
                   and the Sergeant gets a wallet of notes and is going to be
                   a Superintendant, Tadhg's children will be milking cows
                   and keeping donkeys away from our ditches. That's what
                   we have to think about and if there's no grass, that's the
                   end of me and mine.

Fr Murphy: God will ask you questions about this murder one day.

Bull: And I'll ask God questions! There's a lot of questions I'd
                   like to ask God. Why does God put so much misfortune
                   in the world? Why did God make me one way and you
                   another?

Sergeant: Let's go, Father, before I throw up!

Fr Murphy: You'll face the dead man's widow some day, McCabe . . .
                   not here, but in another place.

Bull: Indeed I won't, Father, because she'll have her own facing
                   to do with another man by her side.

                   [Exit FR MURPHY and SERGEANT]

Bull: *[Louder . . . after them]* No, I won't face her because
I seen her and she's a pretty bit and the grass won't be
green over his grave when she'll take another man . . .
A dead man is no good to anyone. That's the way of the
world. The grass won't be green over his grave when he'll
be forgot by all . . . forgot by all except me! *[To MICK]*
There's your other twenty. C'mon Tadhg.

*[BULL pauses a moment. Then gathering himself, he throws
back the remainder of his drink and leaves the pub. MICK
gives the counter a wipe and returns upstairs. Silence.*

*The half-door of the cubbyhole we saw in the first act
swings open, revealing LEAMY. He has been there
throughout the scene. He climbs out and stands centre
stage. We feel that he is in the grip of torturous indecision,
but finally he turns reluctantly to the table and begins
clearing the drinks away]*

[The End]

Big Maggie

This edited two act version of *Big Maggie* was first presented in the Abbey Theatre, Dublin on Monday 21 November 1988.

MAGGIE	Brenda Fricker
GERT	Tina Kellegher
KATIE	Anne Byrne
MAURICE	Seán Campion
MICK	David Herlihy
TEDDY	John Olohan
MARY	Linda Mc Donnell
MRS MADDEN	Maureen Toal
BYRNE	Johnny Murphy
OLD MAN	Eamon Kelly
OLD WOMAN	Maura O'Sullivan
MOURNERS	Bill Monks
	Lynn Cahill
	Collette Hoctor
	Peter Cooney
	Tom O'Brien
PRIEST	Karl O'Neill

DIRECTOR   Ben Barnes
SET DESIGNER   Frank Conway
COSTUME DESIGNER   Consolata Boyle
LIGHTING DESIGNER   Rupert Murray

Big Maggie was first produced by Gemini Productions on 20 January 1969 at the Opera House, Cork.

ACT ONE

Scene 1

[Action takes place in a graveyard. A near middle-aged woman dressed in black is seated on a headstone buttress smoking a cigarette, with her handbag clutched between her knees.

In the background can be heard the sound of earth falling on a coffin. A man and woman, both old, stop to pay their respects. In turn they shake hands with MAGGIE POLPIN]

Old Man: Sorry for your trouble, Maggie, he was a good man, God be good to him.

Maggie: He was so.

Old Woman: He was a good man, if he had a failing, Maggie, 'twas a failing many had.

Old Man: He had a speedy release, God be good to him and that's a lot.

Old Woman: Worse if he was after spending six or seven months in a sick bed.

Maggie: He went quick and that was the way he wanted it.

Old Woman: That was a blessing.

Old Man: *[Emphatically]* That was a lot all right. Make no mistake! We can't all go the way we'd like.

Maggie: We can't.

Old Man: You may say we can't! There's no one can.

Old Woman: He was a cheerful sort of a man.

Maggie: Cheerful is the word.

Old Man: What age was he?

Maggie: He was just turned sixty.

Old Man: He didn't get a bad share of it.

Old Woman: There's a lot never saw sixty.

Old Man: And a lot never will! We must be thankful for all things and accept the Holy Will of God.

Maggie:	We must indeed! Well, I won't be holding you up, if you're in a hurry.
Old Man:	I understand, Maggie. You want your own about you at a time like this. I was wondering if you'd have any notion where Madge Gibbons is buried? There's no stone over her.
Maggie:	I've no idea! Sure isn't one grave as good as another. 'Tis the thought that counts you know!

[Old man and old woman exit and GERT enters]

Gert:	Won't you go over to lay on the wreaths?
Maggie:	I won't.
Gert:	But, Mother . . .
Maggie:	Don't but me now, like a good girl. I'm in no humour for it.
Gert:	I just thought it would be the correct thing to do.
Maggie:	You're not old enough yet to know what is correct and what is not correct. God forgive me if there's two things I can't endure 'tis the likes of them two caterwaulin' about the dead and the other is the thump of clods on a timber coffin. I couldn't bear to watch that gang around the trench and they trying to look sorry.
Gert:	Can I go over to help with the laying of the wreaths?
Maggie:	No! Your brothers and sisters can do that. 'Tisn't that the wreaths will do him any good.
Gert:	Oh, mother, how can you say a thing like that!
Maggie:	It's the truth! God forgive me 'tis a hard thing to say about my own husband, but that's what they'll be saying in the pubs after the funeral. 'Tis what everybody knows. I'm not a trained mourner, Gert. I can't olagón or moan or look for the arm of another hypocrite to support me.
Gert:	He was no saint but he was my father. *[Rebelliously]* I'm going over to the grave.
Maggie:	You will stay where you are. I have enough to contend with without my youngest wanting to desert me in my hour of need. Call Byrne there! He's on the verge of the crowd somewhere.

Gert: *[Calls, in a loud whisper]* Mr Byrne . . . Mr Byrne . . .
[To MAGGIE] Katie has the wreaths in her arms, she's left
to do everything!

Maggie: She's the only one he had any time for! He liked them
sonsy and she's all that. 'Twill be knocked out of her
now though! I promise you that.

*[Enter MR BYRNE. Easy-going with cap and in the act of
putting a pipe in his mouth]*

Byrne: Sorry for your trouble, Maggie. You too, miss.

Maggie: You look it too Byrne. Now I want a six foot high lime-
stone monument, three feet across. Three inches thick.

Byrne: You're the boss, Maggie.

Maggie: You can start tomorrow.

Byrne: 'Tis not customary, Maggie.

Maggie: What isn't?

Byrne: They generally wait the three months before they put up a
stone.

Maggie: Is it *they* will be paying you, or big Maggie Polpin?

Byrne: I don't know that I'll be able to do it tomorrow. I have to
start on a Celtic cross for Fonsie MacMee.

Maggie: How long is Fonsie dead now?

Byrne: Going on the fourteen months. Why?

Maggie: Well, seeing that he's waited so long, he'll wait a few more
days!

Byrne: I don't know, mam. 'Tis commissioned with a bit.

Maggie: Suit yourself. If you won't do it Cornelius Breen will do it
for me.

Byrne: All right! All right! I'll start tomorrow.

Maggie: Good! How much will it be? *[Opens her purse]*

Byrne: Well, I can't say off hand now. There's a lot of things to be
taken into consideration.

Maggie: Six feet by three feet by three inches. You aren't a school boy.

[BYRNE produces notebook and pencil and starts to do some writing]

Byrne: Six feet by three feet by three inches. What's a quarter of eighteen feet?

Gert: Four and a half feet.

Byrne: *[Writing]* Four and a half feet.

Maggie: In the honour of God hurry up! 'Tisn't a supermarket we're putting over him!

Byrne: I don't want to wrong you, mam!

Maggie: You won't, Byrne.

Byrne: *[Does a final bit of reckoning]* I can't do it for a penny less that £70.

Maggie: £60.

Byrne: Sorry!

Maggie: Cash!

Byrne: Oh, now! . . .

Maggie: On the nose.

Byrne: Materials is very dear, mam.

Maggie: £60 now.

Byrne: All right.

[MAGGIE hands him the £60. BYRNE counts it carefully]

Maggie: 'Tis all there, Byrne.

Byrne: I know, but I don't want to wrong you, mam.

Maggie: The day you wrong me, Byrne, is the day you get me pregnant.

Byrne: All the Byrnes, big and small, wouldn't do that, or couldn't do that! We would need softer stone than you, Maggie.

[GERT giggles. In the backround is the hum of the Rosary. MAGGIE produces a slip of paper]

Maggie:	Here is what you'll inscribe on it. 'Tis all made out.
	[Hands him a slip of paper. BYRNE *reads it out aloud]*
Byrne:	'Walter Poplin. Died March twenty-fifth, nineteen-sixty-three. Aged sixty years. RIP.' 'Twasn't hard to make out that.
Maggie:	Hard enough if you were me.
Byrne:	No charge for a little extra. Fill it out a bit.
Maggie:	That's the lot. There's no more to be said.
Byrne:	Well now missus, 'tisn't for me to say but they usually put 'Erected by his devoted wife and family' or 'by his loving wife and family' or some such thing in that line.
Maggie:	Is that a fact! Well, Byrne, there's enough lies written on the headstones of Ireland without my adding to them.
Byrne:	I know moderate men that died, Maggie, and they were sorely missed.
Maggie:	I don't doubt it.
	*[*BYRNE *shakes his head and makes out a receipt]*
Byrne:	One last thing, Maggie. Which way do you want it facing?
Maggie:	I'm easy about that, Byrne, so long as it don't face towards me.
	*[*BYRNE *hands the receipt to* MAGGIE. *Exits shaking his head]*
Gert:	You didn't hate him that much!
Maggie:	Didn't I now!
Gert:	You couldn't hate a person that much! What's going to happen now?
Maggie:	The first thing I'm going to do is call a meeting. And this will be the right quare meeting! There won't be any proposing or seconding! I have a shop and a farm to run and they are going to be run profitably or not run at all.
Gert:	Oh, come off it, there has to be money!
Maggie:	Has there now!
Gert:	Well, he was insured for thousands!

Maggie:	You are getting a bit too forward for my liking. You'll turn out like your father it you aren't careful.
Gert:	That's not fair. I always took your side in everything!
Maggie:	You did because you had to!
Gert:	You're rotten!
Maggie:	You know very well he preferred Katie to you!
Gert:	To you too!
Maggie:	*[Slaps her face]* How dare you talk like that to your mother! I could paint a picture of your late, lamented father that would really shock you! *[Looks with disapproval about her]* This is one place I won't be buried I can tell you that! I'll fix that shortly too. The earth is a bad enough bed *[Indicates cross]* without bedposts like these.
	[Enter two young men, dressed in sombre overcoats with black bands around their arms. The older of the two is Maggie's son, MAURICE. The other is her son MICK]
Maurice:	'Twas a bloody big funeral.
Mick:	They were there from the city of Limerick!
Maurice:	And Tralee.
Mick:	There was a car-load from Cork.
Maurice:	A man with a Dublin accent shook hands with me.
Maggie:	Did you fix with the grave-diggers?
Maurice:	That's all settled.
Maggie:	And the undertaker?
Maurice:	Paid in full! Here's the receipt.
	[MAGGIE accepts receipt. Enter KATIE. Attractive girl in a sexy way, dressed in black though she is. She is about twenty-two]
Maggie:	In the honour of God dry your eyes and don't be making a show of yourself!
Katie:	I'm entitled to cry when my father is dead.

Maggie:	'Tis long before this you should have cried for him!
Katie:	*[Drying her eyes]* Maybe I did.
Maggie:	Your bladder is near your eyes I'm thinking.
Maurice:	Talk easy let ye or we'll be noted!
Maggie:	We're noticed long ago! *[To sons]* Maybe the two of you will turn into men now. Long enough you stood back from him!
Maurice:	That's not fair!
Gert:	What about the times he blackguarded her?
Maggie:	You were no men you didn't haul out and level him.
Mick:	He was a big man.
Maggie:	Wasn't there two of you?
Maurice:	Let me out of it! I was never a man to come between husband and wife, let alone my father and mother.
Maggie:	You let him abuse me!
Mick:	You were well able for him! Anyone that abused you wound up second in the long run!
Maggie:	Wait till I get you home!
Mick:	It was never a home, ma.
Maggie:	Your father saw to that.
Maurice:	Oh, come on for the love of God! We haven't stopped squawking at one another since he died.
Gert:	Maybe now that he's out of the way we might turn into some sort of a family again.
Katie:	That's a terrible thing to say!
Gert:	You were a great one always for closing your eyes at the dirt under your feet!
Katie:	I notice a very courageous line of chatter now that he's safely out of the way.
Maggie:	I'm warning you, miss, to hold your tongue! There are a few changes coming shortly that might not altogether appeal to you.

Katie:	The King is dead! Long live the King!
Maggie:	That's right. Say your piece now because, believe you me, there's a time coming when you won't have much to say for yourself!
Katie:	What are you going to do? Lock me in, is it?
Maggie:	There'll be no need for that! You were always used to the good times! We'll see what you're like when the good times are taken away from you.
Maurice:	This is a terrible way to be conducting ourselves out here in public.
Maggie:	You're right Maurice. Come on away! We have a shop to open.
Katie:	You're not going to open the shop today, surely to God!
Maggie:	Why not?
Katie:	He's only after being buried!
Maggie:	Not another word out of you madam. Come on, all of you! *[Is about to exit]*
Man's voice:	*[Off]* Mrs Polpin . . . Mrs Polpin . . .
Maggie:	*[Peers in the direction of voice]* Who is that?
Gert:	It's Crawford's traveller.
Mick:	Nice time of the day to turn up for a funeral.
Katie:	Better late than never.
	[Enter TEDDY HEELIN. He is a young man, extremely good-looking]
Teddy:	Terribly sorry I'm late, Mrs Polpin. *[He shakes her hand in sympathy]* Sorry for your trouble.
Maggie:	*[Resignedly]* I know that. I know that Mr Heelin. 'Twas good of you to come.
Teddy:	I had to break a journey. It was only by accident I heard about it. I was on my way to Limerick and I pulled up to get some petrol. The next thing you know the attendant said that Walter Polpin was dead. I hardly believed him. *[Takes KATIE'S hand]* Terribly sorry for your trouble, Katie.

Katie: I know that, Teddy. 'Twas nice of you to come.

Teddy: 'Twas the least I could do.

[TEDDY goes and shakes hands with GERT]

Teddy: Sorry Gert.

Gert: Thank you, Teddy.

[TEDDY shakes hands silently with MICK and MAURICE. He then produces a mass card]

Teddy: *[To MAURICE]* Will you take this? *[Notices that MAURICE already has a bundle of same, he hands card to him]*

Maurice: Thanks.

Teddy: Sorry again, Mrs Polpin. If I'd known I'd have dropped everything to be here on time.

Maggie: We all know that.

Teddy: If there's anything I can do. Anything. Don't hesitate to ask.

Maurice: We'd better be going.

Teddy: Listen, I've got the car outside. I can take some of you down.

Gert: *[Moves quickly to his side]* I think I'll go with you.

Katie: So will I. That's if there's room for the two of us, Teddy.

Teddy: Oh, there's plenty of room.

Maggie: No. Katie, you go with your brothers. I'll go with Gert and Mr Heelin. I've a few matters to settle in town, that's if you don't mind waiting a few moments while I look after may affairs, Mr Heelin.

Teddy: I have all day.

Maggie: That's settled then. Let's get out of this place.

[Exit TEDDY holding GERT'S arm. They are followed by MAGGIE]

Maurice: I'm not sure that I care for that fellow.

Katie: Oh, shut up. You're just jealous of him.

Mick: They say he's a right whoresmaster.

Katie: I wouldn't know about that.

[MICK and MAURICE exit. Enter old man and woman still searching]

Old Man: There's no sign of her anywhere.

Old Woman: Maybe 'tisn't here she's buried at all.

Old Man: We can't find Madge Gibbon's grave.

Katie: Ask Mr Byrne. He knows all about the graves around here.

Old Man: Thank you, miss. We'll do that.

Katie: Don't forget to say a prayer for my father while you're praying for Madge Gibbons.

[Exit KATIE]

Old Man: There's no doubt but he left a mighty strange litter behind him.

Old Woman: That last one isn't the worst of them.

Old Man: Yes! There's a bit of spirit there.

Old Woman: Big Maggie Polpin is a dab hand at breaking spirits.

[Enter BYRNE]

Byrne: Good day folks!

Old Man: Good day to you, Mr Byrne! Fine funeral considering.

Byrne: Yes! Considering.

Old Man: They say he left her comfortable.

Byrne: Oh, there's no shortage of money. The shop does a good business and that's as good a farm as ever threw up a cow.

Old Woman: He was a hard man, God be good to him.

Byrne: *[Casually]* There was plenty harder but they got away with it. He was a man I personally liked. She was wrong for him. She married him for the security.

Old Man: He was fond of a woman now and again. That's what they say.

Byrne: And by the way you weren't, that's if you ever got the chance!

Old Man: Who is without a fault, sir?

Byrne: He got his own way always. That's what happened to him. He had the money and the appearance and when you have those you get the opportunities. Still, I liked him. She was wrong for him. Another woman might have made a better fist of him. 'Tis a mistake to fight fire with fire.

Old Woman: They say he drank too.

Byrne: A bottle of whiskey was no bother to him before his breakfast.

Old Man: Or after it.

Old Woman: Whiskey and women. Sure invoices for a coffin.

Byrne: He wasn't the worst of them!

Old Man: Still you must admit now that he sired a noble share of likely men.

Byrne: Don't I know it! Didn't I see his black hair and big jaw on several here today. Maggie was never able to keep a servant girl in the house you know!

Old Man: Is that a fact?

Byrne: Oh, that's gospel! There was no stallion the equal of that man if you'll pardon me saying so, missus.

Old Man: God knows he left a hard woman behind him.

Byrne: She was all right at first. 'Twas the world hardened her. I remember her a handsome girl. She had no real love for him. He was a good catch at the time.

Old Man: She's no sack of oats now.

Byrne: God bless her, she's nicely preserved all right. I won't deny that!

Old Woman: What made him turn from a fine woman like that?

Byrne: Wisha, will you tell me, missus, what turns them all? I knew honest men and upright men, sober men and sane men and every one of them was betrayed sooner or later by a rogue of a dickie, if you'll forgive the expression, mam.

Old Woman: Oh, God save us! 'Tis a hard plight for an honest man.

Byrne: Did God know what He was doing, mam, or didn't He?

Old Woman: God knew.

Byrne: Right you are then! Where does that leave us?

Old Man: As wise as ever! I do often say to myself, why do people be so slow to kiss goodbye to this goddamn world of pains and aches and puking. Hah!

Old Woman: Robbery and hypocrisy and murder from one end of the day to the other.

Old Man: Life is the grimmest loan of all, my friend. The interest is too high in the end.

Old Woman: 'Tis the cross of man, life is.

Byrne: You'll be thankful to be leaving it so.

Old Man: Listen here to me.

Byrne: Yes?

Old Man: Would you by any chance know where the grave of Madge Gibbons is?

Byrne: Which Madge Gibbons now? Was it the Madge Gibbons that was tackled to Donal Summers or was it the Madge Gibbons that was housekeeper for Canon Mackintosh the Protestant?

Old Man: 'Twas the Canon's housekeeper.

Byrne: *[Thoughtfully]* Madge Gibbons that worked for the Canon Mackintosh. Well, now. *[Points with finger]* Down there at the left hand corner you'll notice a wild rose bush. There's a cypress 'longside of it. Madge is wedged between the two.

Old Man: We promised a prayer first for the man they just put under. I fancy he won't be getting many.

Byrne: Well now. I do be here most of the day and you could count on one hand the number that comes to pray. But the man that went under now has no more prayers to get and from the cut of the widow I'd say she won't think of the next world until she enters it.

Old Man:	So long so!
Byrne:	Good luck.
	[Exit old man and woman]
Byrne:	Limestone. Six feet by three feet by three inches. 'Tis a respectable block of stone. 'Twill be there when he's forgotten and 'twill be there when he's rotten and may God have mercy on the poor man's immortal soul!

Scene 2

[Action takes place that night in the Polpin shop. The door is locked. The cash is counted. The blinds are drawn]

Gert:	I'm dying to hear all.
Maurice:	I wish I could be so cheerful.
Mick:	I suppose she's going to tell us now.
Maurice:	She can't keep us waiting much longer.
	[MAGGIE enters]
Maggie:	You can compose yourselves awhile but I'm going to advise you all to be ready for changes.
	[Lights a cigarette]
Gert:	Can I have one?
Maggie:	No.
Mick:	Is it fair to ask if there was a will?
Maggie:	Keep your shirt on. You'll know all in a minute. *Maurice.* Sit down. Did you pay the workmen?
Katie:	They're paid.
Maggie:	Is all the cash there? *[Indicates cashbox]*
Katie:	Yes.
Maggie:	And all the receipts?
Katie:	What's the matter? Don't you trust me?
Maggie:	I trust no one.

Katie: Do you mean I'm dishonest?

Maggie: I never met anyone who admitted to being dishonest so I
                    wouldn't know about those things. Now let you all listen
                    carefully to what I have to say. It concerns each of you. You
                    asked just now, Mick, if there was a will. Well, there wasn't.

Katie: Impossible.

Maggie: There was no will.

Katie: *[Desperately]* But there has to be a will! He always
                    promised me.

Maggie: Promised you what?

Katie: Nothing.

Maggie: More than me maybe?

Katie: I didn't say that.

Maggie: Now there being no will, as I said, that puts me in charge,
                    which is only as it should be.

Mick: If there's no will how can it all be yours? We're all entitled
                    to our share.

Maggie: There's no will because a year ago your father signed over
                    the place to me.

Katie: What!

Mick: I don't believe you.

Maggie: Don't you now. Ring up the solicitor and see what he has
                    to say.

Mick: You're bluffing.

Maggie: The phone is in the shop, lift it. If you don't believe me,
                    you'll believe D'Arcy.

Katie: Sure how could my father do a thing like that?

Maggie: Do I tell lies? Do I? . . . Well, come on, you've known me
                    long enough and you're quick enough to criticise . . .
                    well, speak up one of you . . . Do I tell lies?

Maurice: No.

Maggie:	Right. This time last year I had a talk with your father and he agreed to sign over the place to me. He had good reason to.
Katie:	Did you blackmail him?
Maggie:	You'll learn to bite that tongue of yours miss, when I have a minute to deal with you — and that might be sooner than you think.
Katie:	I asked you a question.
Maggie:	And you'll get an answer. I got no more than my rights. I brought a £1,000 fortune when I came here and I've slaved here for twenty-five years. I don't think anyone here will deny that. *[To KATIE]* Unless of course you would like to put your spoke in.
Katie:	I've nothing to say.
Maggie:	Good.
Mick:	All right. Tell us how much he left anyway.
Maggie:	Death duties, that's what he left — enough to keep me struggling for years to come.
Maurice:	What are we going to get out of it?
Maggie:	You'll get nothing out of it naturally, not yet anyway. You have a roof over your heads. You have good food and you'll have pocket money.
Mick:	*[Scornfully]* Pocket money! You're mad if you think I'm going to stay here for pocket money. Pocket money is for kids. If I'm to stay here I'll want a share. It was all understood that the farm would be divided between myself and Maurice.
Maggie:	Understood by whom? It wasn't understood by me.
Mick:	You had better get it clear, mother. I am not going to be a servant boy any longer. This farm is to be divided and by divided I mean that both halves will be fully stocked with cattle, machinery and working capital together with dwelling house and outhouses.

Maggie:	Obviously you've been talking to someone! You'd never think up all that by yourself!
Mick:	Well, are you or aren't you?
Maggie:	Am I or aren't I what?
Mick:	Going to divide the farm?
Maggie:	I'll have to see.
Mick:	You'll see right now. I'm not going to be fobbed off by any promises.
Maggie:	Mick, I'm in no position to guarantee anything to anybody.
Mick:	In that case you can look for someone else to run the farm. I'm resigning. Are you coming, Maurice?

[No reply from MAURICE]

Mick:	I'm going, Mother.
Maggie:	Well, you know how to turn the knob on the door, boy.
Mick:	Are you coming, Maurice?

[MAURICE does not reply]

Katie:	Maurice, you were spoken to.
Mick:	Are you coming, Maurice, for the last time?

[MAURICE does not reply]

Maggie:	He won't go. He hasn't got the guts of a louse.
Mick:	Maurice?
Maurice:	I'm saying nothing. I've had enough squabbling for one day.
Maggie:	True to form.
Mick:	I'll need money. Not much, and permission to stay the night. I can't go anywhere till morning.
Maggie:	Yes, a good night's sleep is important.
Mick:	Damn you!
Maggie:	Off to bed now like a good boy.

Mick:	My father is a lucky man to be free of you. I'm beginning to have sympathy for him now.
	[Exit MICK]
Maggie:	He'll be back. He knows where his rations come from. Have you anything to say, Maurice?
Maurice:	*[Stands up]* Yes I have!
Maggie:	No time like the present. Out with it!
Maurice:	I want to get married.
Maggie:	You do?
Maurice:	Yes I do!
Maggie:	And do I know the lady of your choice?
Gert:	I know her. She's Mary Madden from Knockliney.
Maggie:	Dan Madden's daughter?
Maurice:	Yes.
Maggie:	Sit down boy.
	[MAURICE sits]
Maggie:	How many cows has Dan Madden? Fifteen or sixteen, is it?
Maurice:	Yes.
Maggie:	And nine or ten other children to be provided for?
Maurice:	Yes. You have your facts.
Maggie:	And where do you expect to live?
Maurice:	Why here of course! Where else would I go?
Maggie:	Where else indeed?
Maurice:	Then it's all right?
Maggie:	Do you know how much money I had when I came as mistress to this house?
Maurice:	You told us. You had a thousand pounds.
Maggie:	And how much has this Madden one?

Maurice: She hasn't anything.

Maggie: And you expect me to hand over the reins after my twenty-five years to a slip of a girl without a brown penny in her pocket?

Maurice: Well, no.

Maggie: Then what do you expect?

Maurice: We could live here with you. A temporary thing, and I could work away on the farm for my wages until . . . well until.

Maggie: Until I kick the bucket! Isn't that it?

Maurice: It's not! All I want is to get married. There's nothing exorbitant about that.

Maggie: Well, you can tell her to find a fortune of £1,500 and I'll consider her proposal.

Maurice: But she hasn't that kind of money and neither have I. At that rate I'll be waiting forever to get married.

Maggie: Go on and marry for love then.

Maurice: I have no money.

Maggie: But if you marry for love you don't need money.

Maurice: So you say.

Maggie: You're only twenty-four. Your father was thirty-five when he married and there were people who considered him young.

Maurice: God Almighty Mother, give me a break! I'm in love with the girl. She's a good girl! You'll like her!

Maggie: I'd like her a lot better if she had £1,500.

Maurice: But what am I going to do?

Maggie: Forget it for the present is my adivce. We'll think about it some other time.

Maurice: Will you consider it some other time?

[Knock at door]

Gert: I'll go.

Maggie:	Stay where you are.
	[Knock at door. MAGGIE exits]
Maurice:	Do you believe her?
Gert:	I believe her — if Mary Madden can't put down the cash my mother won't let her darken the door.
Maurice:	No — I mean about the will.
Gert:	Sure she said it would be easy to catch her out. Oh I believe her all right. She told me once that the worst thing about telling lies isn't that it's a sin but it's such a waste of time trying to wriggle out of it when you're found out.
Maurice:	My father promised me the farm.
Gert:	Mick said it was to be divided.
Maurice:	'Twas promised to me.
Katie:	Is that why you sang dumb when Mick asked you to go away with him — so you could have it all to yourself?
Maurice:	Mick can make up his own mind, it's nothing to do with me.
Gert:	He's our brother isn't he? Are you going to —
Maurice:	We've had enough fighting for one day. It's best if we all mind our own affairs.
Katie:	Well you're a cool one I'll say that for you. But you haven't a hope in hell of getting married unless my mother can jingle out the wedding march with the Madden's £1,500.
Maurice:	Yerra, shag off! Now that the old fella's dead there'll be a quick stop to your gallop. This time last year you got everything your own way, and the rest of us mightn't have been around for all he cared.
Gert:	Stop it the pair of you, this is getting us no place.
Katie:	Where's there to get. *[To MAURICE]* Give us a fag.
	[MAURICE ignores her. She takes a cigarette from MAGGIE'S packet by the till]
Maurice:	Why in Christ's name did he have to sign everything over to her!

Gert: A year ago. And he never let on.

Katie: A year ago. Moll Sonders.

Maurice: What about her?

Katie: You remember the time she caught him with Moll?

Gert: I don't believe that. I don't believe he ever had anything to do with Moll Sonders.

Katie: You remember our beloved mother was supposed to go to see that doctor in Dublin?

                   [Others nod]

Katie: She left here in a hired car at eight o' clock one night. She was to stay over night. You two and Mick had gone into town to a dance. I went to bed early that night because I was dying from the night before.

Maurice: I remember.

Katie: She didn't go to Dublin at all. She got the driver to turn round after dark and came straight back here. If I had known I could have tipped my father off.

Gert: *[Shocked]* You knew Moll was with him?

Katie: I knew she had called to see him just after I went to bed but I knew nothing else. It could have been for anything. It could have been for the loan of money. You all know he couldn't say no. Besides her husband was in England and he wasn't sending her anything.

Gert: You'd swear black and white to save him.

Katie: I would and what about it!

Maurice: Oh, shut up Gert. Get on with the story.

Katie: Moll arrived about ten o' clock. They spoke in whispers but I knew who it was. About twenty minutes after Moll's arrival I heard someone tiptoeing past my door and going on up the stairs to my father's room.

Maurice: My mother!

Katie: I opened my door and peeped out and I saw the back of
               her just outside my father's door. I nearly dropped dead.
               There was nothing I could do. She burst in the door and
               caught them red-handed.

Maurice: Can you be sure?

Katie: Look! I saw Moll Sonders running down the stairs in her
               pelt and my mother after her. Is that enough for you?

Gert: He was nothing but an animal.

Katie: Oh shut up. I didn't blame him.

Maurice: My God, you're as bad as him.

Katie: For the love of God. My mother didn't sleep with him for
               years and when she did I doubt if she was any good to him.

Maurice: Here now, I'm not going to let you talk like that.

Katie: Oh, grow up! I was at Cloonlara Races with him once and
               he was in the bar swopping yarns with a crowd of his
               cronies. I remember him to say that he was married for
               eighteen years and he never once saw his wife naked!

Gert: You can't talk like that. It's terrible. Stop her, Maurice.

Katie: The bother with you is that you never tried to understand
               my father. All those men in the bar that night had the same
               story. They didn't know I was listening. The wives were too
               damn good. Damn them, they thought it was a sacrilege to
               fornicate with their own husbands.

Maurice: I've given you up long ago but I never dreamed a girl of
               your upbringing could even think like that, not to mind
               talk. You're past understanding.

Katie: Maybe I am but I'm not deaf and I am not blind to what's
               happening about me like the two of you are.

Gert: I'm not going to listen to any more of this.

Katie: Suit yourself.

Maurice: Was that what led to his signing over everything to her?

Katie: Of course it was. I know that he went on an awful booze
               after that again.

Maurice: I remember that and I remember D'Arcy called and went upstairs with Byrne and my mother.

Katie: That's it. Byrne was the witness. She has us where she wants us now. Here she comes.

Maggie: *[Entering]* Nellie Riordan at the door. She'd pray for the deceased and say the stations — which would take her a lot less time than she kept me at the door. Well, there's no need to ask what you were talking about, but I can tell you that your conversation was as big a waste of time as mine was with Nellie.

Maurice: Look, Mother, I'll go up and see if I can talk some sense into Mick.

Maggie: Yes, do that.

Maurice: And you'll definitely consider what I asked you another time.

Maggie: Trust me, Maurice. For years before he died your father drank and spent most of what we made here. It couldn't go on, I had to stop it. We'll work hard now and get the place going again. Go along now, God is good.

                 [Exit MAURICE]

Katie: You haven't an earthly notion of letting him marry that girl. Why didn't you tell him the truth?

Maggie: He'll get over her. Besides he's a good worker and help is hard to get. There's plenty of time for him to marry.

Katie: Jesus, you're a hard case!

Maggie: How dare you take the holy name in my presence!

Katie: 'Twas from you I picked it up.

Maggie: I'll let that ball over the bar for the moment. I'll tell you about the arrangements I have for you shortly. It might drive some of the steam out of your engine.

Katie: I can't wait!

Maggie: Believe you me, you'll be sorry you said that.

Katie: Free country you know.

Maggie:	Shut up you rip or I'll strike you. *[To GERT]* Gert, you are to leave the kitchen and come into the shop with me unless you want to get married too.
Gert:	Oh no! I'd see more of Crawford's traveller in the shop, wouldn't I?
Maggie:	You like him?
Gert:	He's a lamb.
Maggie:	He's a good-looking scoundrel all right. I'll say that for him. You can talk away to him in the shop but otherwise you are to have nothing to do with him, you hear?
Gert:	I hear.
Maggie:	Good.
Katie:	I'd like to ask a question.
Maggie:	Go ahead.
Katie:	If Gert is to go into the shop and if you and I are already in the shop who is going to do the kitchen?
Maggie:	Can't you compose yourself! Amn't I coming to that. You think I make these arrangements on the spur of the moment.
Katie:	We don't want three of us in the shop.
Maggie:	I couldn't agree with you more so I've decided that you are to do the kitchen.
Katie:	Not a hope!
Maggie:	You'll do the kitchen, Gert deserves a turn in the shop.
Katie:	I won't do the kitchen!
Maggie:	I have no intention of making a game out of it. We're both too old for this 'I will' and 'I won't' business. From tomorrow morning you will begin work in the kitchen. If you don't I'll send you out of this house a pauper. How would you like that?
Katie:	I could always make a living.
Maggie:	*[Meaningfully]* I'm afraid you could.

Katie: Oh, by God, now we're getting the innuendos. Could you tender an addition to that implication?

Maggie: Will you take it now or will you wait till you get it?

[Enter MICK wearing an overcoat]

Maggie: I must say you weren't long coming back.

[But MICK ignores her and goes directly to where the cashbox is. He is about to take it up in his hands when MAGGIE intervenes]

Maggie: Here what in hell do you think you're doing?

Mick: I need a few pounds. It's my due.

Katie: Don't leave, Mick! Don't give in to her. 'Tis what she wants.

Maggie: *[To KATIE]* Keep out of this.

[MICK snatches the cashbox from under MAGGIE's hand. He opens it and looks inside]

Mick: *[To KATIE]* How much is in here; £100? £120?

Katie: There's £97 in cash.

Maggie: Don't touch that money.

Mick: *[To MAGGIE]* Keep back or I'll give you a belt. I swear to God I will!

[He takes the money from the cashbox and puts it in his pocket]

Maggie: If you don't put back that money this instant you will never darken the door of this house again.

Mick: Don't worry. You'll hear no more from me.

Maggie: I mean it.

Mick: And I mean it.

Maggie: Just remember Mick, that wherever you go, you won't do better than home.

Mick: *[To KATIE]* I'll want a loan of your car to take me to the station. You can collect it in the morning.

Katie:	You're welcome. The keys are in it. Good luck, darling!
Mick:	Goodbye Katie. Goodbye Gert.
	[Exit MICK]
Gert:	*[A little appalled]* Is he gone for good?
Maggie:	Never mind him for the present. *[To KATIE]* Now you see the trouble my family is causing me. You can forget about your car too if the kitchen doesn't suit you.
Katie:	It's my car.
Maggie:	Who pays the tax and insurance and who buys the petrol? It's the property of the house.
Katie:	You wouldn't take away my car!
Maggie:	My car if you don't go into the kitchen. The kitchen will do you good. I have big plans for you!
Katie:	Get one thing into your head right now, my mother. You will not dominate me.
Maggie:	Of course you know what you can do, don't you? You can blow any time you want! If you won't do what you're told I don't want you around.
Katie:	All right. I'll call your bluff. I'll start in the kitchen tomorrow morning.
	[She moves to go]
Maggie:	You, stay where you are. I'm not finished with you. Our little conference is only beginning. *[To GERT]* You go out to the kitchen and put on a fry for me and see that you don't burn the rashers like you did this morning! Move!
	[Exit GERT. MAGGIE returns to her seat having locked the shop door]
Maggie:	Sit down there. First things first. Did Johnny Conlon propose to you a year ago?
Katie:	He did!
Maggie:	Is he still to the good?

Katie: He is.

Maggie: Is he still interested?

Katie: He is, but I'm not.

Maggie: Why didn't you tell me the time he proposed to you?

Katie: It wasn't important and besides I turned him down. He's not my type.

Maggie: You'll marry him and you'll marry him within the next three months which is more.

Katie: You're a howl!

Maggie: Laugh while you can.

Katie: I laughed before this you know.

Maggie: You're twenty-two years of age and you haven't a penny to your name without my say so.

[KATIE still laughs]

Maggie: *[Calmly]* You'll marry him.

Katie: *[Getting over laughter]* I told you before he's not my type.

Maggie: *[Coldly]* What is your type?

Katie: I don't know what you mean.

Maggie: I think you do Katie!

Katie: This is worse than a court-room.

Maggie: The night of the creamery social, you went to the dance with Gert.

Katie: So did three or four hundred other girls.

Maggie: We'll forget about those! It's you and Gert that concern me. You sat with Gert throughout the dinner but after the dinner you went to the public bar.

Katie: I did! But if you already know all this, why do you need to ask me?

Maggie: *[White with temper locates a sweeping brush]* You see this brush?

Katie:	*[Losing some of her assurance]* I do.
Maggie:	As sure as your father is in his grave tonight, I'll break this brush across your back if you give me another single word of back-chat.
Katie:	*[Afraid]* Yes, mother.
Maggie:	Now, you went to the public bar?
Katie:	Yes, mother.
Maggie:	With whom did you go, Katie?
Katie:	Gert told you.
Maggie:	Gert did not tell me. Gert doesn't know. Now, with whom did you go to the bar?
Katie:	Let me alone, can't you. I'm all torn up after the funeral and I can't take any more of it.
Maggie:	Tell me the name of the man who was with you?
Katie:	What man?
Maggie:	*[Angrily]* His name!
Katie:	Toss Melch.
Maggie:	So it was Toss Melch.
Katie:	Yes.
Maggie:	Was his wife with him?
Katie:	No.
Maggie:	Where did you first meet him?
Katie:	Last year at another social.
Maggie:	So you've known him a year?
Katie:	Yes.
Maggie:	And before the night of the social, how many times did you meet him?
Katie:	Four or five times.
Maggie:	That night in the bar, how many drinks had you?

Katie:	Just a few. Two or three. I forget exactly.
Maggie:	You had six halves of gin. Now at half-past eleven, this married man booked a room in the hotel and he went upstairs immediately. When he left, what did you do?
Katie:	I had a dance or two.
Maggie:	And after that?
Katie:	Well, I went upstairs, to go to the ladies' cloak-room.
Maggie:	But there is a ladies' cloak-room downstairs.
Katie:	It was crowded. Mobbed. I tried to get in a few times but it was next to impossible.
Maggie:	And how long were you in the upstairs ladies' cloak-room?
Katie:	*[Convincingly]* It was before twelve when I came down. I'm sure of that.
Maggie:	No it wasn't! You came downstairs at five minutes to two just before the social ended.
Katie:	*[Fearfully]* It's a lie! It's a lie!
Maggie:	It's not a lie! You went upstairs at quarter to twelve and you didn't come down till five minutes to two. Now what were you doing upstairs for nearly two and a quarter hours?
Katie:	Nothing. I was doing nothing, Mother.
Maggie:	Katie, you were seen. Two days after that night I had an anonymous letter from someone who signed themselves a friend. *[Viciously]* Tell me what you were doing upstairs for two and a quarter hours.
Katie:	Nothing. Nothing I tell you!

[MAGGIE advances upon her and seizes her by the hair of the head. Swings KATIE around so that she faces her]

Maggie:	You went into the room booked by Melch and you stayed there with him for two and a quarter hours. What were you doing?

[KATIE is silent. MAGGIE slaps her face]

Maggie: Have I raised a whore? *[Screams]* Have I raised a whore? Have I?

[Still holding her by the hair she shakes her]

Maggie: Tell me what you were doing in that room or I'll beat you so that your own sister won't know you.

[Lifts her by hair off chair and still holding her hair she forces her to kneel on floor]

Katie: I was committing a sin with him.

Maggie: Louder. I can't hear you!

Katie: I was committing a sin with him.

Maggie: And it wasn't the first time?

Katie: No. No. I couldn't help myself.

Maggie: *[Letting go of her hair]* Get up will you.

[KATIE is still kneeling and sobbing]

Maggie: Get up and act like a woman.

[KATIE rises slowly]

Katie: Sure you won't beat me?

Maggie: No! I won't beat you. I was mistaken about you! I thought you were more brazen, more of a woman. You're still a child.

[MAGGIE lights herself a cigarette and offers one to KATIE who takes it cautiously. MAGGIE lights it for her]

Maggie: Sit.

Katie: What are you going to do with me?

Maggie: Why should I do anything to you when you've already disgraced yourself?

Katie: Will I be left stay here?

Maggie: You will under certain conditions.

Katie: I agree Mother.

Maggie:	Since Johnny Conlon proposed to you has he been in touch with you at all?
Katie:	He has tried. He salutes always and he wrote a few times.
Maggie:	Write back to him. Tell him you would like if he called, that you are down and out after the death of your father and whatever else occurs to you.

[MAGGIE goes towards exit]

Maggie:	Bring me the letter before you put it in the envelope. If we play our cards properly he may propose to you again. Tell him from me, thanks for his Mass Card, that I appreciate the thought. Will you tell him that, Katie?
Katie:	Yes.
Maggie:	Before I forget it, first thing in the morning, go down to the station and collect your car.
Katie:	Are you going somewhere?
Maggie:	No, I'm not going anywhere, but it just occurred to me that it's about time I learned how to drive.

Scene 3

[Action takes place in the shop of MAGGIE POLPIN. It is a country shop where almost everything is sold.
The time is three months later, mid-morning.
MR BYRNE is at the counter with a message bag in his hand.
Behind the counter is GERT. She is adding items on a piece of paper]

Gert:	*[Half to herself, half to BYRNE]* Pound of butter, bread, washing soap, toilet soap, sugar, tea, bacon . . . Did I give you the tobacco?
Byrne:	You did! I have it here in my pocket. Are you all right, Gert?
Gert:	I am . . . thanks.
Byrne:	Are you sure?
Gert:	*[A trifle impatiently]* Thanks. I can handle it.
Byrne:	I hope so.

Gert: That's the lot. Will you keep an eye here for a few minutes till I check these prices with my mother?

Byrne: Fire away but don't be all day. I've work to do. Oh, Gert, tell your mother I was asking for her.

Gert: I will. I won't be a jiff!

[Exit GERT. BYRNE locates his pipe and lights it. Enter TEDDY HEELIN]

Teddy: Good morning!

Byrne: Not a bad morning.

Teddy: Not bad. It's nice outside. Seems to be clearing.

Byrne: You're with Crawfords, aren't you?

Teddy: That's right. I had no idea I was so well-known.

Byrne: How are things around the country?

Teddy: Things could be better but then again they were often worse. Anyone around?

Byrne: Gert will be out in a minute. Just went in to check a few prices with the mother. I suppose you meet all kinds in your travels?

Teddy: All kinds. Believe you me, my friend. All kinds.

Byrne: I can imagine.

Teddy: Oh, you'd be amazed.

Byrne: Travelling is a job I wouldn't like.

Teddy: You never know till you've tried.

Byrne: I daresay that's true.

Teddy: Is Gert in the shop now?

Byrne: Oh yes! For the past few months, since the father died.

Teddy: He went quick, didn't he?

Byrne: Sudden. The heart.

Teddy: Sudden is the best way.

Byrne: So they say.

Teddy: How is the missus since Polpin died?

Byrne: Bearing up well, mind you.

Teddy: The oldest girl Katie. Where is *she?*

Byrne: Married.

Teddy: You're not serious.

Byrne: Fortnight ago. Fellow a few miles down the road, big
                 farmer.

Teddy: God knows 'tis hard to believe. I thought she'd knock a
                 few more berls out of the world before she dropped anchor.

Byrne: 'Twas a surprise all right.

Teddy: She was a lively girl.

Byrne: Lively?

                 [They laugh]

Byrne: Her husband's a very nice man. Bit advanced of course.
                 Would want to get his gun oiled I'd say. You'd be a likelier
                 man now for taking a crack at a target like Katie.

Teddy: And how do you know that I didn't score a few bulls-eyes
                 there before this?

Byrne: It wouldn't surprise me! It wouldn't surprise me one bit,
                 my friend. Here's Gert.

                 *[Enter GERT still checking list of messages. When she
                 notices TEDDY HEELIN she shows her delight]*

Gert: Teddy Heelin! How are you?

Teddy: Couldn't be better thanks be to God. How're you?

Gert: Fine! Fine! I'll be with you in a minute, Teddy, as soon as I
                 finish here. *[To BYRNE]* The whole lot comes to two pounds
                 one.

Byrne: *[Locating money]* Two pounds one. Here you are.

                 [GERT accepts money and deposits it in cash register]

Byrne:	Did you tell her I was asking for her?
Gert:	Who?
Byrne:	Your mother!
Gert:	I did!
Byrne:	What did she say.
Gert:	She laughed.
Byrne:	What kind of laugh was it?
Gert:	What do you mean?
Byrne:	Well, was it a short laugh or a long laugh. Was it a wicked laugh or a gay laugh?
Gert:	She seemed to enjoy it.
Byrne:	Good. Very good!
Teddy:	How's business, Gert?
Gert:	Not bad. She has a big order for you.
Teddy:	Good. That's what we like to hear.
Gert:	He's a right charmer, Mr Byrne. He gets orders everywhere.
Byrne:	I wouldn't doubt it!
Teddy:	'Tis the quality of the goods, not me, Mr Byrne!
Gert:	Oh, go on out o' that! Everyone knows he's a ladies' man! They say he has more sex appeal than any other two travellers.
Byrne:	That's no bad mark against him. I could use a bit of it myself.
Gert:	When are you going to take me out, Teddy Heelin?
Teddy:	Do you want your mother to horse-whip me?
Gert:	Oh, she lets me out now. I can go wherever I like and with whom. She knows I'm sensible.
Teddy:	If you're serious, I'll take you out some night.

Gert: I'm serious. It was always Katie he noticed before, Mr
           Byrne. He used to call me the baby.

Byrne: She's no baby now, my friend, but by God she has the
           equipment to feed one.

Gert: Mr Byrne!

Teddy: I won't disagree with you there.

Gert: Mr Byrne, didn't I hear you say a while ago that you had
           work to do?

Byrne: I get the message! I won't stand in the way of romance.
           [Is about to exit] But I'll tell the two of you this for your
           own good. Don't be too hasty to say anything to Maggie.
           She'll be slower than a parish priest to give a blessing to
           what doesn't suit her.

           [Exit BYRNE]

Gert: Don't take any notice of him. He's nice really!

Teddy: Are you serious about my taking you out?

Gert: I am!

Teddy: I'd have asked you for a date long before this but I didn't
           want to cross your mother.

Gert: Are you afraid of her too?

Teddy: Being afraid of her has nothing to do with it. She's one of
           my best customers and I don't want to fall out with her. In
           my job you have to be cautious. What time do you want
           me to call tonight?

Gert: Tonight! What time would suit you?

Teddy: After the post goes out I'm free. I could call any time after
           that.

Gert: Half-seven be all right?

Teddy: I'll be there. Your mother won't mind?

Gert: No! She likes you. In fact she said so. Oh, she says you're
           a bit of a playboy and that you'd want watching. But she
           does like you.

Teddy: Where do you want to go?

Gert: I don't mind.

Teddy: We can decide that when I call.

Gert: You won't get fresh with me now. I wouldn't like that! I'm not that kind. You had better know in time.

Teddy: I know you're not. That's why I'm so keen to take you out.

Gert: The novelty I suppose.

Teddy: No! I think about you in a very special way. I wouldn't want to do anything to hurt you.

Gert: I believe you.

[TEDDY takes her hand]

Gert: Stop it you eejit! Do you want someone to walk in!

Teddy: I'm no saint! But I suppose you know that.

Gert: I've heard things.

Teddy: You don't have to worry. I wouldn't harm a hair of your head. I just want to be near you. To hear you talking, laughing, whispering!

Gert: *[Laughs]* Whispering?

Teddy: Yes! Whispering! Something tells me that you're a terrific whisperer and if there's one thing I love it's to hear a nice girl whispering!

Gert: You're a scream!

Teddy: Whisper something to me now!

Gert: *[Indulging him]* What will I whisper to you?

Teddy: Anything you like.

Gert: All right then. *[She whispers in his ear]*

Teddy: *[Upon hearing it he draws away]* I'm shocked. I'm scandalised! How could you say such a thing!

Gert: But all I said was it's a nice day.

Teddy: That's it! It's not just a nice day! It's a lovely day! It's a beautiful day, or do you know the day we have?

Gert: I do. It's Tuesday!

Teddy: *[Shakes his head]* NO! No! No! Today is the day that Gertie Polpin made her first date with Teddy Heelin. *[Takes her hands again]* Now, whisper something nice to me!

Gert: Such as?

Teddy: Such as — you like me.

Gert: *[Whispers]* I like you.

Teddy: And I like you too. *[Sings]* 'Those eyes are the eyes of a woman in love. And oh how they give you away'. I don't suppose you'd be inclined to whisper 'I love you'.

Gert: It's a bit early for that, isn't it?

Teddy: Oh I suppose so. *[Seriously]* But when the day comes that you say that, I will be a very happy fellow.

Gert: Be sure and be here at half-seven.

Teddy: Is that an order?

Gert: It is!

Teddy: Well, I can tell you, Miss Polpin, that it's the most valuable order I've had since I became a commercial traveller. I suppose you intend to reform me?

Gert: Well, since you ask, it's only fair to tell you that it's the highest notion in my head. Do you mind?

Teddy: I'm going to enjoy it.

Gert: It won't be easy.

Teddy: Come on, give us a kiss and I'll give you a free pair of garters.

Gert: You're terrible.

    [They kiss briefly. Enter BYRNE. TEDDY *draws back from* GERT*]*

Byrne: Do you know what I forgot?

Gert: We don't know but why don't you tell us?

Byrne: Raisins. Seedless ones. Did you get them in? You hadn't them the last time. *[To TEDDY]* I like a bun, sir, with raisins in it.

Gert: *[Produces a packet of raisins]* Here they are. I hope you enjoy the buns.

Byrne: Are they seedless?

Gert: As far as I know.

Byrne: How much?

Gert: Two shillings.

            [BYRNE hands over the money and examines the raisins]

Byrne: *[To TEDDY]* Aren't they cheap now, sir, considering the long journey they come.

            [Exit BYRNE]

Teddy: Bit nosey, isn't he?

Gert: The local encyclopaedia. I'd swear he's a notion of my mother.

Teddy: Ah, go on.

Gert: I'd better call her.

Teddy: Yes, better, I've a good few calls to make before the post. I haven't much time.

            [GERT goes to exit of shop and calls]

Gert: Mother . . . Mother . . . Crawford's traveller is here.

Teddy: You make me sound like a stranger.

Gert: You're anything but.

Teddy: How is your mother by the way?

Gert: Never better. She drives now, you know.

Teddy: Oh, when did she learn?

Gert: Katie taught her before she married.

Teddy: Your man told me about Katie's marriage. I must say I was surprised.

Gert: The wild ones always settle down quickly once they make up their minds.

Teddy: Is she happy?

Gert: She seems to be. He's very wealthy, you know. I wouldn't marry him of course. He asked me once, the first time after Katie turned him down.

Teddy: I wouldn't have taken 'no' for an answer.

Gert: How are you sure the answer would have been 'no' when you never asked?

[Enter MAGGIE. She is dressed in a smart bright frock. She looks younger. Her hair is neat and orderly and she is well made up]

Teddy: Hello, Mrs Polpin.

Maggie: *[Charmingly]* Hello, Mr Heelin.

[Shakes hands with him]

Teddy: So Katie got married?

Maggie: She did indeed. We would have invited you to the wedding but we decided to keep it strictly family so soon after the funeral.

Teddy: Of course.

Maggie: You look well.

Teddy: I must say, Mrs Polpin, that I've never seen you looking better and that isn't just sales talk!

Maggie: Do you hear that, Gert, he's looking for an order already.

Teddy: Seriously, Mrs Polpin, I would appreciate the order right away. I'm a little behind schedule.

Maggie: Well, it's all made out for you together with your cheque.

Teddy: Good.

Maggie: Like a good girl will you go back to the kitchen and keep an eye on the dinner.

Gert: OK. See you Teddy.

[Blows him a kiss without MAGGIE's noticing. Exit GERT. MAGGIE goes behind counter and returns with cheque while TEDDY who has taken receipt book from attache case is writing out a receipt. MAGGIE hands him order and cheque]

Maggie: Here you are, Teddy. It's a wonder some nice girl hasn't scooped you up before this.

Teddy: The right one didn't come my way yet.

Maggie: You had a grand chat with Gert before I came out?

Teddy: Yes, Gert is a very nice girl.

Maggie: She's young, Teddy.

Teddy: She's a woman, Mrs Polpin. Your receipt.

Maggie: Call me Maggie. We've known each other a long time. The size of the order you've just received should show you what we think of you here. I regard you as a friend of the family and that's why I'm asking you to stay away from Gert.

Teddy: You make things very awkward for me.

Maggie: I think we know each other. At least I know a good deal about you. I know for instance, that you're no cock-virgin with innocent dreams of romance.

Teddy: By the Lord, you don't mince words.

Maggie: I don't believe in mincing words.

Teddy: Good. We can be candid then but how candid is the question.

Maggie: Be as open as you like. That's the way I like it.

Teddy: The first part of what you said is true but you're wrong about the second part. I'll be honest with you and tell you that I've asked Gert if she would like to come out tonight and she's willing, and I'm glad, very glad, because I genuinely like her. What's more I could easily fall in love with Gert.

Maggie: You're a good-looking fellow! No doubt she finds you attractive, I honestly don't blame her.

Teddy: Thank you.

Maggie: You really are attractive and I can see how easy it would be for any woman to fall for you. She's too young for you. You're too assured and too experienced for my Gert. You say you have honourable intentions. Does this mean that you intend to marry her one day?

Teddy: Marry? To tell you the truth I hadn't thought about marriage but with a girl like Gert it would have to be marriage — wouldn't it?

Maggie: You mean that she wouldn't allow you in to bed with her unless you married her?

Teddy: I wish you wouldn't put it like that but I suppose you're right.

Maggie: Let's be honest. Do you desperately want to go to bed with her?

Teddy: Well, that wouldn't be unnatural if I loved her.

Maggie: But it boils down to the same thing, doesn't it . . .?

Teddy: It does not! It's more than sex. You want me to be honest. I will! I've fancied other women and wanted to make love to them and I often did. As far as sex is concerned I've never really been satisfied. I don't mean I've been frustrated but something has been missing.

Maggie: And you think that the thing that has been missing is a nice girl like Gert?

Teddy: Well . . . yes.

Maggie: So that's what you think of the women you slept with. They gave you the lot and all you can say is there was something missing.

Teddy: You make it sound different than it really is.

Maggie: Maybe it's your conscience that's at you!

Teddy: That's not it exactly.

Maggie: Tell me what it is exactly.

Teddy: Are you blaming me for past mistakes?

Maggie: I'm not and you know I'm not!

Teddy: I don't usually let a woman talk to me this way.

Maggie: It seems to me that for all your women you're not very happy.

Teddy: *[Pause]* Meet a woman, make love to her and gone the next day — what does it all add up to? I used to promise myself that each time would be the last time. But I was tempted. Maybe this time it's the right one.

Maggie: Gert?

Teddy: Maybe not. Oh, she's a beauty but maybe I need someone more . . . mature.

Maggie: Someone with experience.

Teddy: Yes . . . it's a bit of a game sometimes.

Maggie: Romance is for young ones, Teddy. I had my share of it and then I married the wrong man. For ten years he didn't sleep with me. In the end I didn't want him, but it was a strange and terrible way for a healthy woman to live. I wouldn't tell you this but I feel we understand each other.

Teddy: Ten years . . . that's a long time.

Maggie: Sometimes it didn't matter.

Teddy: And other times? . . . I hate to think of anyone being unhappy. There's no reason for it now, you're free.

Maggie: No one knows that better than me.

Teddy: You can have the things you want now. Do what you like. Who's to stop you?

Maggie: No one.

Teddy: God knows I'm not giving you advice — I've been in too many scrapes myself and there were times things happened I was sorry for afterwards.

Maggie:	Sure, that's what life is. That's the way men are. I know.
Teddy:	Of course you know. There aren't many women with your understanding and honesty, Maggie. You won't be offended if I say this . . . Sometimes a man and a woman, they have the same need — the same longing. It can happen quickly, they don't need any romantic games. They know. Sometimes a man can see a woman and want her more than anyone ever before. He wonders if she thinks the same?
Maggie:	She might — if she thought the same about him.
Teddy:	How would he know?
Maggie:	That would be for him to find out.
Teddy:	You're a remarkable woman. I'd like to really understand you.
Maggie:	You will.
Teddy:	All the times I've come in here and talked to you and I never really knew you until now. That sounds like sales talk but I mean it — I don't think I've felt this way with any woman before. I don't know what it is about you — but for once I'm not sure of myself.
Maggie:	Oh, but I want you to be yourself, Teddy.
Teddy:	When can I see you . . . alone I mean?
Maggie:	When do you want to see me?
Teddy:	The sooner the better. Tonight!
Maggie:	Tonight, then.
Teddy:	Tonight.
Maggie:	What time?
Teddy:	Whatever time you say.
Maggie:	Nine o' clock. I'll have everything done by then.
Teddy:	It's such a long way off!
Maggie:	It will be worth waiting for. *[TEDDY makes to kiss her]* Go now.

Teddy: Oh God! What about Gert?

Maggie: Let me worry about Gert. Her fancies don't last.

Teddy: Perhaps I should tell her that I'm breaking our date?

Maggie: No! Don't worry about it! I'll take care of everything. You'd better finish off your calls. I don't want you to be late.

Teddy: I won't be late. Till tonight then.

Maggie: Till tonight.

          [Exit TEDDY]

Maggie: *[To herself]* Till tonight.

          [End of Act One]

ACT TWO
Scene 1

[The shop is empty. BYRNE passes the door, pauses, then enters. He knocks on the counter, changes his mind and exits. As he does MAURICE enters from house and sees him go. MAURICE carries a bucket. He crosses to the meal sack. Then he bends down behind the counter for the meal scoop. BYRNE returns and again knocks on the counter — unaware of MAURICE]

Byrne: *[Surprised]* Good evening.

Maurice: Good evening.

Byrne: I was passing.

Maurice: So I saw.

Byrne: I came in.

Maurice: Can I get you something?

Byrne: Herself.

Maurice: My mother?

Byrne: Who else?

Maurice: I'll call her. *[At door]* Mother, Mr Byrne's here to see you. She'll be with you in a minute. *[Pause]* I'm only getting a few scoops of meal for a weak ewe. We're near closing.

Byrne: The shop's doing well this past while.

Maurice: Could be better.

Byrne: How about your end — the farm?

Maurice: Could be worse.

Byrne: That's something in these hard times.

Maurice: Hard times is right, according to my mother anyway.

Byrne: She'll know best.

Maurice: None better — according to herself.

Byrne: Your mother is like strong medicine, Maurice — hard to take sometimes but 'twill do you good in the long run.

Maurice:	How long is the long run?
Byrne:	You mean the young Madden one I suppose? A nice little girl. I do see the two of you some evenings heading for Kelvey's Wood.
Maurice:	Sometimes you see too much, Mr Byrne.
Byrne:	Could be. But I've more time on my hands now with the style of tombstones getting smaller. I often sit on the graveyard wall remembering past generations, contemplating the present one and having a shot at where the future generation will come from.
Maurice:	It's easy for you to make jokes but if you were in my shoes you'd wonder if there was going to be any future generation at all.
Byrne:	If I was in your shoes, Maurice, I'd learn how to lace them myself and not have my mother always tying them for me.
Maurice:	You don't know my mother.
Byrne:	I wasn't talking about your mother, I was talking about you.
	[MAGGIE enters]
Maggie:	Maurice, did you mark that meal on a slip of paper and put it in the till?
Maurice:	I did. Would you like it signed by the Minister for Agriculture?
Maggie:	If it meant keeping my books straight for the tax man I would.
	[Exit MAURICE]
Maggie:	Well, Byrne?
Byrne:	Good evening, Maggie.
Maggie:	Oh, good evening to you too. Was it you I saw walking up and down past the door earlier?
Byrne:	Could be.
Maggie:	What's the matter with you now?
Byrne:	I won't put a tooth in it. I came to put my cards on the table.

Maggie: You'll have to postpone the game, Byrne, because I'm otherwise engaged as of now.

Byrne: I won't keep you two minutes.

Maggie: *[Thoughtfully]* Two minutes. OK. Fire away!

Byrne: Now that I have my chance I don't know where to begin.

Maggie: For a beginning, I may tell you that you're doing a lot of arsing around here lately.

Byrne: I don't deny I'm around here more than I should.

Maggie: I've noticed you for the past few weeks like a gander that would badly want to gattle a goose.

Byrne: I suppose that's one way of putting it.

Maggie: Only the other night I was saying to myself, Byrne is looking a bit hot and bothered and says I Byrne is behaving more like a jackdaw than a monumental sculptor.

Byrne: You've had your say. It's my turn now. I have £4,000 in the bank.

Maggie: I'm not surprised the prices you charge for headstones.

Byrne: I'm a man of sober habits although I take a drink if the occasion calls for it and I have no objection to a woman taking a drink either. I'm a steady worker and there is a wide demand for my work. I'm a good Catholic and I does the Nine Fridays regular. I never missed Mass in my life and there's no year I don't earn more than would keep a family in comfort. I am told by folk that should know that I am the best monumental sculptor around these parts.

Maggie: You're a monumental eejit if you ask me.

Byrne: Well, will you or won't you?

Maggie: Will I or won't I what?

Byrne: Marry me.

Maggie: Marry you?

Byrne: Yes.

Maggie: Were you ever at the zoo, Byrne?

Byrne: I was, the year of the Eucharistic Congress when I was in
                Dublin. That was 1932. I was a fine young man then. But
                what has the zoo got to do with it?

Maggie: Well, Byrne, if you were at the zoo, you know what a
                baboon is?

Byrne: *[Innocently]* I dare say I do.

Maggie: Good for you, because, Byrne, I would sooner be buckled
                to a baboon than be buckled to you.

Byrne: You're an insulting woman! Oh, a baboon would suit you all
                right. The bother is, Maggie, that no self-respecting mother
                of a monkey would consent to a son of hers marrying you.

Maggie: You gave me my answer. I'll hand it to you, Byrne.

Byrne: Die, Maggie, and I'll give you a Celtic Cross for nothing.
                [To TEDDY who is entering] Good night to you, sir.

                [Exit BYRNE]

Teddy: *[Laughs]* What was that all about?

Maggie: Believe it or not, Teddy Heelin, I've just had a proposal of
                marriage.

Teddy: And did you say yes?

Maggie: I've had my fair quota of marriage, thank you.

Teddy: Where's Gert?

Maggie: She's gone to see Katie.

Teddy: Good. Was she disappointed when I didn't show up?

Maggie: Very. *[As TEDDY advances]* Wait until I lock the door.
                Anyone could walk in. I like a man who is punctual.

                [He goes to her]

Teddy: I thought about you all day. I made several mistakes when
                I was totting my returns in the hotel and that's something I
                never do. I missed you.

                *[He puts his arms around her and kisses her. She responds
                and they draw apart to survey each other]*

Maggie:	You're so uncomplicated.
	[They kiss again]
Teddy:	Let's not stay here much longer. Can we go upstairs?
Maggie:	What's the rush? Sure we have all night. Come here.
	[He takes her in his arms and kisses her, fondling her as he does so. She doesn't resist. Enter GERT silently. TEDDY is kissing MAGGIE passionately]
Gert:	Mother!
	[TEDDY looks around foolishly and sees GERT. He breaks with MAGGIE]
Gert:	Was that the reason you sent me with the groceries to Katie?
	[MAGGIE does not reply]
Gert:	*[To TEDDY]* You know what she did? She sent me off to Katie's twenty minutes ago and told me to hurry back again, that she wanted me for something else. I know you played about but I had no idea you would stoop to do a thing like this!
Teddy:	Believe me, Gert, I'm . . . I . . .
Gert:	Two-faced isn't the word for you and as for you Mother. You let him kiss you!
Maggie:	Aren't you forgetting something?
Gert:	What do you mean?
Maggie:	I'm single now, the same as you.
Gert:	I hate you!
Maggie:	Any girl with an ounce of sense would thank me. If you had your own way you'd make a complete wreck of your life.
Gert:	And is it how you think it's not wrecked now?
Maggie:	A small scratch is all you got. 'Twill be healed in a week at your age.
Gert:	You're welcome to him, you're a rotten pair! The two of you.
	[Exit GERT]

Teddy:	You shouldn't have done that.
Maggie:	Do you think I liked doing it?
Teddy:	Christ, it was a cruel thing to do.
Maggie:	She'll get over it and she won't travel the same road I did. You won't get the chance to treat her like the dirt under your feet. The man I married behaved exactly the way you are behaving now. Everyone told me he'd change when he got married but he didn't change. If anything he got worse.
Teddy:	You made a fool out of me.
Maggie:	You did it to yourself. You think that every woman is dying to fall into your arms.
Teddy:	You shamed me. No matter what I am or what I was, no one has the right to do that to another human being.
Maggie:	Don't give me that tripe about human beings, because that's the biggest lie of all. If a man or woman hasn't self respect they have nothing. You should know that because you are nothing, you have nothing, and God pity you, you never will.

Scene 2

[Action as before.
The time is the evening of a day almost a year later.
MAGGIE is behind the counter. KATIE with a pram is on the outside.
MAGGIE is totting a list of messages]

Maggie:	The whole lot amounts to six pounds one and seven pence.
Katie:	I'll pay you now. Himself will call for them tonight. *[Handing over a note to MAGGIE]* You'll throw off the one and seven pence anyway!
Maggie:	I'll throw off nothing. I'm running a shop, not a relieving office.
	[MAGGIE holds the note against the light and then puts it in the till. Gives KATIE her change]
Katie:	What will you do with all the money you have?
Maggie:	I have no money!

Katie: Ah, stop!

Maggie: *[Simply]* I have no money but I have my health. How would I have money with supermarkets sprouting up like daisies?

Katie: There's no one your match!

Maggie: If I was looking at that baby from here till doomsday I couldn't make out who he takes after.

Katie: There's no telling at that age. He's like his father sometimes and sometimes like his mother.

Maggie: I happen to know the mother and there's no likeness. Maybe he is like his father. I wouldn't know about that of course.

Katie: God Almighty, you're a terrible woman!

Maggie: Katie, a woman would want the character of Saint Brigid in this country to get away with a seven months' birth.

Katie: Meaning what?

Maggie: Meaning you're no Saint Brigid. What are you feeding the child?

Katie: The pasteurised of course.

Maggie: There's no nature in children since they stopped the breast-feeding. Women these days don't seem to know what tits are for. In my day every child was fed from the breast.

Katie: Well, if you were fed from the breast, mother mine, it didn't give you much nature.

Maggie: That tongue of yours will get you into trouble one of these days. 'Tis a wonder your husband doesn't take a stick to you.

Katie: If he did I'd cripple him with a poker.

Maggie: I don't doubt you.

Katie: Did you hear anything from Gert since she left?

Maggie: Not a word.

Katie: Maurice had a letter from her.

Maggie: If he had he never said it to me.

Katie:	She told him in the letter to tell you nothing.
Maggie:	What's she at over there?
Katie:	She's doing nursing. She's in a flat with Mick.
Maggie:	Nursing . . . See now, wasn't I for her good?
Katie:	What happened the night she ran away?
Maggie:	It was the beginning of her education. I gave her the matriculation, you might say. 'Twas the best bit of schooling she's ever likely to get.
Katie:	She left in a terrible hurry. Maybe it was a bit too severe.
Maggie:	Nothing is too severe for what she'll meet in this world.
Katie:	Have you any notion of letting Maurice get married?
Maggie:	To the Madden one, is it?
Katie:	Who else?
Maggie:	The day she lobs up £1,500 on the counter I'll be the first woman to dance at her wedding.
Katie:	Mary Madden is a nice girl and Maurice has his heart set on her.
Maggie:	Pass that information on to the bank manager and see how much you'll get for it.
Katie:	I'm telling you in time. Maurice won't wait much longer. He's been pushed as far as he'll go.
	[Enter BYRNE]
Maggie:	Well! Well! Well! Byrne! I thought we'd never again see you.
Byrne:	I'm like my monuments, Maggie! Takes more than a gale of wind to flatten one of them. Katie, how are you?
	[He shakes hands with her]
Katie:	I'm fine, Mr Byrne, thank you. How's yourself?
Byrne:	Carrying the day the best I can, Katie! Maggie, throw us out a half quarter of tobacco. *[Puts money on the counter. Looking into pram]* Is this the garsún? God bless the child! He's like you, Katie.

Katie:	Thank you, Mr Byrne.
	[BYRNE continues to peer at the child]
Katie:	*[To MAGGIE]* Have you any notion of getting in a few girls to help you?
Maggie:	My experience of girls is that they only come in the way.
Katie:	Very funny. You'll never manage all the work alone.
Maggie:	Meaning of course that I should let that Madden one in.
Katie:	She's a topping worker, Mother, and a marvellous milker.
Maggie:	Well if she is, she won't milk my cows. In the honour of God, Byrne, give the child a pound or two. Do you see him with his lousy half-crown giving it to the child.
Byrne:	Silver is the done thing.
Maggie:	If that's your case, show me up a fiver and I'll change it into silver for you.
Byrne:	You're very free with other people's money. I bet you weren't so liberal with the child yourself.
Katie:	Good for you, Byrne!
	[Enter old man and woman who were seen at the church-yard earlier]
Old Woman:	God bless all. *[They acknowledge her salute]* Give us a pound of sugar, please, Missus.
Maggie:	Shag off out of here and get your sugar where you get your tea. There's no profit on sugar. Here's your tobacco, Byrne.
	[Old man and woman are examining the baby]
Old Man:	Look at the small child. Well! Well! Well!
Old Woman:	Is it a boy or a girl?
Byrne:	*[Accepting the tobacco]* That's no way to talk to those old people. You should be ashamed of yourself.
Maggie:	The same applies to you if you don't like the situation here.
Byrne:	God bless you but you have a heart of limestone.

Maggie:	Wouldn't I want it, to be dealing with the likes of you.
Old Man:	He's a healthy little rascal 'faith! What do you call him?
Katie:	He's called Micheal after his Uncle Mick.
Old Man:	How's Mick doing now?
Katie:	Very well, thank you.
Old Woman:	And Gert? What way is Gert?
Katie:	She's doing nursing.
Old Man:	A nurse is handy. No family should be without a nurse.
Old Woman:	*[To KATIE]* And yourself, missus. How're you keeping?
Katie:	Fine, thank you.
Old Woman:	Is he showing any signs of a tooth?
Maggie:	Shag off out of here and don't be addling us. If you want any more information buy the papers.
Old Man:	*[To old woman]* Come on away, woman!
	[The old woman moves towards the door. The old man takes a final look into the pram]
Old Man:	Well, there's one consolation anyway. He don't look one bit like his grandmother.
	[Exit old man and old woman]
Katie:	You had that coming.
Maggie:	Those two came for gossip. 'Tis their passport into the public house. Byrne, do you want anymore messages?
Byrne:	*[Raises his hand]* Don't worry, I'm leaving. So long, Katie!
Katie:	Goodbye, Mr Byrne.
Byrne:	By the way, Maggie, that offer I made you still stands.
Maggie:	Like the monuments you're always boasting about, Byrne, 'twill be standing forever. *[Exit BYRNE]*
Katie:	What does he mean by that?
Maggie:	He wants to marry me.

Katie: Ah, go on!

Maggie: He proposed.

Katie: If he has any sense he'll stay single.

Maggie: Maybe 'tis your own story you're telling.

Katie: What difference does it make to me now — I'm tied and there's damn all I can do about it. Still, it could be worse. I have my own car and I handle the money. I have independence and that's more than most wives have.

Maggie: And you have that eejit of a servant boy drooling after you like a stud greyhound. Watch yourself of that fellow! He wouldn't be long cooling your radiator.

Katie: I can't help it if I excite his interest.

Maggie: Cut that out now, do you hear? I'm still capable of coming outside the counter and putting you in your place.

Katie: You wouldn't dare touch me now, my mother.

Maggie: I'll touch you if I see the need for it. Be certain of that.

Katie: What really brought me here this evening was to talk to you about Maurice.

Maggie: Will you ever learn to mind your own business?

Katie: He asked me and I made him a promise I'd talk to you.

Maggie: Go on!

Katie: Johnny would secure him for the money if you hand over the place.

Maggie: What kind of an eejit do you take me for? I haven't the place a year yet and you want me to hand over already.

Katie: It's not fair to Maurice, Mother. How could he pay back the money he borrowed if he wasn't boss?

Maggie: It would be less fair to me, Katie. As far as I can see everyone is anxious to forget about that.

        [Enter MAURICE. MAGGIE produces a cigarette and lights it]

Katie: Give us a fag.

Maggie:	Buy your own. You have more than I have.
Maurice:	Well?
Katie:	*[Hopelessly]* I've done my best, Maurice.
Maurice:	Mother, a year ago, you told me to wait, that God was good. God has turned out to be no good but maybe that's because you're not giving Him much of a chance.
Maggie:	I can't understand why you have this awful rush on you to get married. I look after you well, don't I? If I was dead you'd need a woman to help you run the place. There would be some sense to that but there's no sense at all to this carry-on.
Maurice:	You asked me to wait and I've waited a whole year, and meaning no disrespect, I would much prefer Mary Madden to look after me than you.
Maggie:	Wait just one more year and I'll see what way the land lies then.
Maurice:	That's what you told me last year and by the looks of things that's what you'll be telling me every year till I'm an old man.
Maggie:	I know I asked you to wait, Maurice, and now I'm asking you to wait again. Try to have patience.
Maurice:	My patience is at an end.
Maggie:	I'm for your own good. Must I always be telling you that? For your good I am! If you take my advice, Maurice, you'll be in no hurry to give up your freedom. 'Tis only now I know what freedom means.
Maurice:	But, Mother, I can't wait any longer. Unless you grant me permission I'll join Mick and Gert in England. It's no bother to get married there.
Maggie:	Oh, no bother at all, and less bother to live in one dirty room all your life. What sort of a job do you think you'll get . . . You have no training for anything but the pick and shovel. Here you're the same as the best in the land and there's something thought of you.

Maurice: Johnny Conlon will put up the security for the money you want. He'll do it the minute you agree.

Maggie: And then Dan Madden's snotty-nosed daughter takes over here. Nothing doing! 'Tisn't the Colleen Bawn you're playing with.

Maurice: All I know is that I'm in love with Mary Madden and I want to marry her.

Maggie: And will you be in love with her when she's trying to rear three or four children in a poke of a flat! When she starts to get fat and irritable and has no time to dress up or do her hair? When her teeth start getting bad, when her belly is swollen and her nose starts to run?

Maurice: Don't say that!

Maggie: Every one of her mother's seed and breed had snotty noses and big backsides like bullocks before they were thirty.

Maurice: Jesus! I don't have to listen to this.

Maggie: When you have four or five kids and start to run short of money, you'll remember me and your fine car and your wardrobe of clothes and you'll curse Mary Madden for the conniving little vixen she is. What makes you think she sees anything in you? If you were a labouring man she wouldn't pass you the time of day.

Maurice: You'll get no one to work as I did. Who's going to look after the land and milk the cows?

Maggie: I'll sell the cows and I'll let the land. You'll be the one to lose, not me.

Maurice: I've given my whole life to that farm and this is what I get in the end.

Maggie: Maurice, I don't want you to leave but you'll have to choose between me and Mary Madden.

Katie: Mother, he means what he's saying.

Maggie: So do I!

Maurice: I'm going now to tidy up the yard and that's the last stroke of work you'll ever get out of me. *[Exit MAURICE]*

Katie:	God, but you're hard.
Maggie:	'Tis the hardness of concern. Always remember that about me.
Katie:	To be fair to you I know now that there's an element of truth in what you said to him.
Maggie:	Aha! My first convert!
Katie:	Oh no, I'm not! Things can be like you say but they needn't be if you let him stay here. *[KATIE turns pram towards exit]* Mick is gone. Gert is gone and now Maurice is going and he won't come back.
Maggie:	Have a good look and see if you can see any tears on my face.
Katie:	But you'll be all alone here, completely alone.
Maggie:	Don't be too sure. What's to stop me from marrying Byrne? He has £4,000 in the bank.
Katie:	Don't be ridiculous.
Maggie:	What's ridiculous about it? Byrne won't live for ever and if Byrne goes there's plenty left for another one after him.
Katie:	You're not serious?
Maggie:	Go on home, girl. Go on home will you and cook your husband's supper.
Katie:	Mother, do you have any feeling at all for Maurice?
Maggie:	I have! I have it for all of you. That's why I never let any of you have your own way. If I hadn't love I wouldn't care.

Scene 3

[Action takes place as before. The time is that night. MAGGIE is seated on a high stool with a leger in front of her, speaking into a telephone]

Maggie:	Maisie, just one more call, please. Will you get me the Whacker Flynn like a good girl and for the love of God, don't announce me. I know the whole country is looking for the whore. And I know why so be nice and sly and

hand him over to me without a word. I'll hold on. *[Pauses]* Hallo! Hallo Whacker, I'm fine thank you but I'd be a lot finer, Whacker, if you paid your bill. *[She listens]* Last month you said you'd send it tomorrow and the month before that, you said you'd send it tomorrow. It's here now for six months and as far as I can see you have no intention whatsoever of paying it. *[Listens]* No need, I'll spare you the price of a stamp. I'll be over in half-an-hour for it so you'd better have it for me. *[Listens]*

[Enter a girl in her early twenties. She wears a coat which gives her a look of simplicity. MAGGIE notices her but says nothing]

Maggie: *[To phone]* I've heard all that before, Whacker and if Mary Josephine is pregnant again 'tisn't me that's to blame for it. *[Listens]* Ah, sure we all know that you can't get blood out of a turnip but it would be an easy matter for me to drive a cow out of your stall. *[Listens while she takes stock of the newcomer]* All right, I'll give you one hour but if you aren't here by then I'll be over and I'll note you. *[Listens]* And good luck to you too boy. *[MAGGIE puts down receiver]*

Mary: Good evening, Mrs Polpin.

Maggie: Good evening.

Mary: *[Shyly]* I suppose you don't know me.

Maggie: How do you know I don't?

Mary: *[Uncertainly]* Well, we've never met before.

Maggie: That's true.

Mary: I was going to sympathise with you at the graveyard when your husband died but I didn't want to be forward.

Maggie: I'll be with you in a minute. *[Pause as Maggie comes from behind the counter]*

Mary: I suppose I'd better introduce myself.

Maggie: No. There's no need for that. To tell you the God's honest truth, I was kind of expecting you.

Mary: Were you? I suppose I should have called before this but I'm terribly shy. *[Gushes on]* It was in my head to call several times but when I was about to start out, something always stopped me. I don't know what it was. I just couldn't bring myself to do it.

[MAGGIE places chair]

Maggie: Sit down there where I can have a good look at you.

[MARY goes and sits on chair, uncomfortably]

Mary: I'm really astonished that you should know me, especially since you never laid eyes on me before.

Maggie: I had a good look at you when you came into the shop. I said to myself, who's this one now and before I had that phone out of my hand, I knew you and I knew your business. This is Mary Madden, I said to myself and by all the laws her mother isn't far behind her.

Mary: She's outside talking to Maurice. They made me come here. I didn't want to but they made me. Maybe I shouldn't have come at all but it had to be done I suppose.

Maggie: Yerra, don't upset yourself, girl. Well, you came as soon as you could. You must be three or four months gone, now, and that's the only card you have, poor child. Three or four or maybe it's only two? *[MARY doesn't answer]* Ah, come on now Mary, you can tell me.

Mary: *[Astonished and hurt]* How did you know?

Maggie: Anyone would know! 'Tis what I would call the inevitable.

Mary: *[Incredulous]* How do you mean, the inevitable?

Maggie: You don't show, I'll say that for you but you can't keep it in forever can you?

Mary: No, I can't.

Maggie: God help us, child. You can't. 'Tis no fun to be carrying a child without a licence.

Mary: You're not angry, so?

Maggie: Angry? Why would I be angry? What has it got to do with me? I have no right to be angry with you.

Mary: Oh, so that's the way is it?

Maggie: That's the way it is exactly. Whenever I see a poorly-off
               slip of a girl like yourself now knocking around with a
               well-off young lad like my Maurice I do be on the look-
               out for it, so to speak.

Mary: I can see that I'll get no sympathy from you.

Maggie: Well, if sympathy was all you wanted I'd give you an
               assload of it but I would say you're after more than
               sympathy.

Mary: God you're clever.

Maggie: You shouldn't have put all your eggs in one basket.
               Wouldn't I be in a nice way now if I had signed over
               to Maurice before this! I'd be a walking tragedy, girl,
               depending on the likes of you for my breakfast, supper
               and tea and afraid of my sacred life for fear I might do
               something or say something to offend your ladyship.

Mary: That's not true at all.

Maggie: God blast you, girl, I've seen the poor innocent bitches
               pressurised into handing over to daughters-in-law. Mighty
               Amazons of women who built empires and then gave it all
               away to be treated like dirt, to be reduced to scutter.

Mary: Stop exaggerating.

Maggie: *[Dropping all subtlety]* Wouldn't it be a marvellous victory
               for you. Think of it! You could be the lady of the manor
               and could have the mother to advise you and maybe your
               young sisters to help you in the shop and those wasters
               of brothers of yours running around the farm. Was that
               the way you thought it would be?

Mary: I wanted Maurice. I want him more than ever now and
               what's his by right.

Maggie: You tried hard all along until you thought of the final
               number. But then you figured that I was no sop on the
               road and you knew that you'd have to go for a goal if
               you were to have any kind of a chance.

Mary: What people say about you is true. I'm going out and I'll send my mother in to you.

Maggie: Did you weigh up the odds well before you decided to surrender yourself? Did you? What were the odds? This house, this farm and all that go with them for one minute of madness in the back of a motor car? Oh, I know your type well, you brazen bitch, and I'd wipe the floor with you before I'd give you the washing of a plate here.

Mary: *[Coldly]* By Jesus, you won't wipe the floor with me. I can tell you that right now. I'm not one of your children, your softies that can be bullied or frightened.

Maggie: I know that well but I knew it all along the way you held on to him. You have gumption enough to get what you want but by the Lord God, you won't get it off me.

Mary: Don't be so sure of that.

Maggie: And don't go too far with me because as soon as I'd look at you, I'd give you a pound weight between the eyes and there's no one would blame me. I'm entitled to respect under my own roof.

Mary: *[Changing her tactics]* You're right. I shouldn't talk back to you in your own house.

Maggie: Amn't I the lucky woman though, that it is my own house! Amn't I? You'd give me short shrift if I had signed over to Maurice.

Mary: Maybe we started off on the wrong foot!

Maggie: It isn't the way we started that matters my girl. It's the way we finish.

Mary: I couldn't agree more. My mother has something to say to you. *[Exits]*

Maggie: You had a right to bring your grandmother too for all the good it will bring you.

Mrs Madden: *[Off]* Well?

Mary: It's like talking to a brick wall, Ma.

Mrs Madden: By Jesus, she hasn't bargained with Hanna Madden.

Maurice: Leave it, Mrs Madden. You'll get nowhere with her.

Mrs Madden: We'll see about that. *[Entering]* Well, Maggie Polpin, have
                  you decided what you're going to do about my daughter?

Maggie: She's your daughter, mam!

Mrs Madden: Answer my question, Maggie Polpin! What do you intend
                  to do about my daughter.

Maggie: As I said before, my good woman, she's your daughter.

Mrs Madden: But your son is to be the father of her child!

Maggie: That's his look-out, not mine.

Mrs Madden: I'm not leaving here till there's a settlement. We have a
                  right to that!

Maggie: You have a right to nothing.

                  [MRS MADDEN folds her arms and assumes a belligerent stance]

Mrs Madden: Come down off your high horse, missus, or you'll be the
                  sorry woman. I'm telling you now and I'm giving you
                  advance notice that you're up against the wrong crowd
                  in the Maddens. The grass will grow on the road to your
                  shop from the boycotting we'll give you.

Maggie: You boycott me or let a member of your family stand
                  outside my door and I'll fix them quick. *[MAGGIE produces
                  double-barrelled gun from under shop counter]* Do you
                  see this?

Mrs Madden: Jesus!

Maggie: Let one of your breed so much as stand within an asses'
                  roar of my shop and you'll be picking buckshot out of
                  their arses for the next ten years.

Maurice: There's no point in going any further with her. I know her!
                  I should have known better than to expect you to have any
                  success with her. We'll be in England in a week and we'll
                  be married and I'll never be back here again! *[He goes to
                  MARY's side]*

Mrs Madden: I'm not yielding an inch till she does the right thing by my
                  daughter that I reared well. I didn't rear her for England.

Maggie: Maurice, if you have any sense you'll have no more to do with this gang. Break with them now, boy, because 'tis the last chance you'll ever have!

Maurice: What about the child?

Maggie: Let Mrs Madden here figure that one out. I'm sure it would be no bother to her. *[Mrs Madden advances threateningly]*

Maurice: Mrs Madden! *[To MAGGIE]* Have you any bit of consideration at all. *[Near to tears]* Have you any feelings? You are driving me out of my father's house, out of the home where I was born and reared. *[To all]* I hate going! I hate it! I hate it! I hate it! I'm a grown man and yet I have nothing, no money, no land, no home. *[Slowly repeats through clenched teeth]* Who can I thank for it all? My own mother!

Maggie: Maurice, I'm not forcing you to go.

Maurice: You have an answer for everything. *[To MARY]* I'll get the car around and drive you home. I won't be a minute. *[Exit MAURICE]*

Mary: Now I see what you're really like, I'll give him the happiness you never gave him.

Maggie: Maurice was always happy here till you came along but you've come around him nicely between the pair of you.

Mrs Madden: By Jesus I heard you were rough, Maggie Polpin and I heard you were tough but hard is what you really are. You're as hard as nails. I swear there isn't a belly in the hospitals of Ireland that would throw out a gallstone half as hard as you!

Maggie: Yerra shag off outa that. I'm sick of you! The cheek of you to come barging like a circus elephant into my house!

Mrs Madden: I wouldn't waste my breath on you! Come on. *[Exits MRS MADDEN]*

Mary: If he ever gives in, in the years ahead and wants to come and see you, I'll stop him and when you're on your death-bed I'll stop him and I'll get him to stop the others too! I can do it!

Maggie: I know well what you can do but devil the use any one of them will be to me when I'm on my death-bed.

[Exit MARY. MAGGIE closes the door after her and walks down to the front of the stage. The light closes in behind her]

Maggie: I'm alone now but I'm free and not too many women can
say that. But I need not be alone and that's the beauty. A
woman need never be alone as long as men crave what she
has, and that never gives out. When I married, God help me,
I was only a slip of a thing. I hadn't an idea what I was
facing. You think someone would have warned me but
they all stood back and let me go ahead. Marriage was the
only safe place for a young girl they said. You'll have a
home, you'll have security. My marriage was a life-long
battle with me always on the defensive and my husband
trying to bend my will right from the beginning. Oh there
were words of love. Blandishments. Didn't he call me a fair
mare one time and he drunk. 'Your a fair oul mare,' he said
and he spent after being astride me for the one bare minute.

You know the first time, indeed the only time, I saw a
penis, before I was married, was on a young garsún and
he bathing in the river. It was a harmless little tassle of a
thing and sure me, poor innocent me, didn't I think that
they were all like that till the first night of our honeymoon.
You'd think my love-life already trimmed and stunted to
the marrow would have to endure no more but the awful
truth was that my sex-life, my morals, my thought, word,
and deed were dominated by a musty old man with a black
suit and a roman collar and a smell of snuff. I was suffocated
by the presence of that old man. He sat in his confession-
box, withering and me not knowing which way to turn for
guidance. Do you know my husband never saw me naked?
He never saw me white and shiny and shivering without
one blemish on me from head to heel. I must have seemed
as frigid and cold to him as a frozen lake. How could I thaw
with my upbringing and my faith, my holy, holy faith.
Maybe that's what drove him into the arms of Moll Sonders
and God knows how many others. My body might say one
thing but my faith always said another and my instincts were
no match for that faith.

Oh I curse the stifling, smothering breath of the religion
that withered my loving and my living and my womanhood.

I should have been springing like a shoot of corn. I should
have been singing with love, tingling, but my love never
grew. 'Tis a wonder that I didn't surrender entirely to
insanity in a country where it was a mortal sin to even
think about another man. And there was another man.
He was dark-eyed and quiet and he passed me a hundred
times on the road and he'd say 'How ya there, Maggie?' and
he'd give one of the cows he was driving a little tip in the
back with his ashplant and I'd say 'Fine thank you, Martin,'
and he'd pass on. I saw him blush once but he never uttered
one word of love to me in all those years and I longed for
him. I craved him in my dreams and I thinking how lovely
it would be to walk with him through the dewy fields. But
he did blush.

And yet I never beamed at that man or set my cap
for him or held his hand or winked at him or even gave
him the faintest clue as to the names I called him and we
cuddled together in those dreams. My curly ram, my sugar
stick, my darling.

He's dead now that easy-going man and my husband is
dead and all too soon I'll be dead but I can have anything
I want for a while anyway. By God I can have any man in
Ireland if there's a man I fancy and who fancies me. There's
still time to fulfil myself. From now on I'll confess my
fantasies to a lusty, lanky man with muscle, a man brimming
with sap and taspy, a man who'll be a real match for Big
Maggie Polpin. The weal of the chastity cord is still around
my belly and the incense is in my nostrils. I'm too long a
prisoner but I'll savour what I can, while I can and let the
last hour be the sorest.

[The End]

Glossary

A chroí (achree): my dear
Amadán (amadawn): fool

Banbh (bonham): piglet
Bean an Tí: woman of the house (housewife)
Bóithrín (bohareen): laneway
Buachall: Boy
Buaileam sciath (bualam ski): Braggadoccio

Cnáimhseáil(cnabsheal): grumbling
Cumar: ravine, usually with a stream flowing in it
Cúram: family (responsibility)

Dúidín (doodeen): clay pipe

Fústar (fuastar): fuss
Faldals: Keepsakes

Garsún (garsoon): boy
Gomaral (gomeril): simpleton
Go mbeirimid beó: may we be alive (this time around)
Grámhar (gradhbhar): loving-tender

Leanbh (Leanav): child
Lorgadawn: puny creature

Mar dhea (moryeah): pretence

Óinseach: fool
Olagón (ollagone): wail

Púca: ghost, pooka
Raiméis: Nonsense

Sciath: basket
Sea (sha): yes
Sláinte: health
Smohawnach: sensitive or smoldering

Tamaill: a while
Tatháire: cheeky person (scrounger)